WOMEN
Unveiled

WOMEN
Unveiled

13 Stories of Restoration to Power, Purpose, and Peace

ERIKA ETIENNE

purposely
created
PUBLISHING

Special discounts are available on bulk quantity purchases by book clubs, associations and special interest groups. For details email:
sales@publishyourgift.com
or call (888) 949-6228.

For information logon to:
www.PublishYourGift.com

To

Marvis Etienne

Your unwavering love and support helped

me fulfill one of many dreams, and

you are living proof that God answers prayers.

For

Lynn Braxton

Because if it weren't for the foundation

you set for Shakira and me, I don't know that

I would have had the strength to rely on

God to get me through my darkest hours.

CONTENTS

INTRODUCTION
by Lynn Braxton

Have you ever found yourself asking the question, "Why me?" When you are faced with problems on the job, financial difficulties, marital discord, difficulties managing your children and their busy schedules, health challenges, or just trouble dealing with the daily struggles of life, do you ask, "How can I find the strength to get through this? What is my purpose in life? Why is there no peace in my life?" As women, we are natural caretakers and nurturers. We want to fix the things that are wrong in the lives of our family members or on our jobs; however, we can feel overwhelmed if we're not able to resolve these problems. In addition, when we need time for ourselves, feelings of guilt can arise.

You may think God has forsaken you or you may question what your purpose is on earth. If you're tired of trying to resolve these types of matters on your own and desire solutions that have worked for others, my hope is that you will find what you need here. *Women Unveiled: 13 Stories of Res-*

toration to Power, Purpose, and Peace chronicles the journeys of women who, at some point in their lives, have felt as you may feel right now. In their chapters, they explain their dark times, their pitfalls, and their quests to discover the Lord's gifts of power, purpose, and peace.

By reading this book, you will acquire a clear understanding of the divine power and authority that God has placed in you to manifest your true purpose in life. The tears you've cried, the prayers you've sent forth, and the troubles you've experienced are not in vain. God has already equipped you with three magnificent gifts—power, purpose, and peace— to help you maneuver through all of life's challenges. Sometimes, we lose sight of these gifts and begin to wonder whether we are deserving of or will ever receive God's blessings. This book will help you to ***understand the gifts*** the Lord has already blessed you with and will ignite a fire in you to move beyond your circumstances.

Each woman in this book has experienced some degree of defeat, but she persevered and recognized that God was truly at the helm of her journey. While she may not have recognized His presence as she was going through a challenge, she would later learn valuable lessons that have shaped who she is today and solidified the purpose God had for her all along.

Finally, with the knowledge you obtain from reading *Women Unveiled*, you can begin to ***utilize your gifts*** for God's glory! May the Lord empower you with wisdom as you read through each chapter of this book, which will prepare you to fulfill the calling He has placed on your life. Then, you will never again question why weapons were formed against you, but will fully believe that they cannot prosper (Isaiah 54:17). I implore you to be excited about all of what God has in store for you to experience! Enjoy!

POWER, PURPOSE, AND PEACE

by Shakira Williams

God, where are You?
Feeling so alone
Wandering
Wondering
Needing someone to talk to
My plans failing
Give me a sign
Feeling empty
No direction
No satisfaction
What is this?
Trial after trial
Tribulation after tribulation
Feeling powerless
When will this end?

God, where are You?
With me?
Still want to use me?
Please!
Forgive me!
I'm ready to say yes
Yes to Your will
Not mine
But Yours be done in my life
What is the reason?
Why have I been chosen?
To endure this hurt
To endure this pain
Lord, I'm ready for a change
Hear me as I call on Your name!
I'm no longer the same.

God, where are You?
Are You listening?
Are You nearby?
I'm ready to testify
How Your love and Your grace
Your mercy and Your faith
Have sustained me
Anoint me oh God
Walk with me
For the journey You have designed just for me

In power, in purpose, in peace!
I'm ready!
I hear You Lord
Yes, I'm ready!

FIVE PRINCIPLES TO LIVE YOUR BEST LIFE

by Angela Blair

Growing up with a Navy father, I moved around a lot, but found Virginia to be home. After graduating from high school there in 1997, never in a million years did I think that, sixteen years later, I would return in the middle of a divorce from a toxic marriage.

For years I was perceived as a woman who could handle anything thrown her way, but underneath the day-to-day stress I was crumbling. However, on the brink of it all, my connection with God strengthened, enabling me to stand tall as my authentic self. What I learned through the dissolution of my marriage is that change is only difficult when we're attached to the story. The toxicity of my marriage required me to confront the biggest abuser in my life—ME. Coming from a place of strength, I was ready to dive in and reclaim my life.

With God by my side, the five principles below, used at different times in my life, guided me through the dark clouds:

1. **Trust your instincts.**

2. **Do what you believe is right for you.**

3. **Ignore more, because you can't please everyone.**

4. **Apologize.**

5. **Count your blessings, then bless others.**

PRINCIPLE 1: TRUST YOUR INSTINCTS

As a woman, you must listen to your intuition because it is your greatest asset. One thing you need to comprehend is that God gave that vision to you. Not everyone will see nor will they understand the moves you make, and this will be a test of discernment. I've been through this several times when it was necessary for me to ignore the opinions of others and trust the vision God gave me. My first test will forever be my reference for what is possible with a strong sense of faith.

In 2001, I reached a point in my military career that allowed me to retrain out of the Security Forces career field I had been in. I had a strong feeling that Information Technology would be prevalent in the future, so therefore decided that Communications would be best for my family. Typically, once you're in Security Forces you're locked in. No one thought I would make it out, not even my spouse at the time, but my faith was strong. I was determined to block out the voices of the pessimists and focus solely on overcoming the obstacles in my way. My ASVAB (a military career qualification test) score did not meet the requirements so I retook the test. The rescore was again not high enough, so I enlisted the help of my Chief and humbly requested he write me a letter of recommendation. Surprisingly, he did. Bear in mind, this is not the standard request a twenty-one-year-old Airman asks of an E-9. Most males are terrified to speak to a Chief, despite the open door policy that is preached, and there I was, a young female asking for help.

In my mind—and I live by this today; in fact I'm always hammering this into my daughters' heads—the worst anyone can say is NO. With that mindset, I refuse to allow a YES to pass me by. I submitted my package then waited. The standard protocol is that you have two chances, and if you don't make the first board, there's one more opportunity. Boy, was I persistent. The retraining team knew who I was because I called every third week of the month like clockwork to check on my status; however, due to 9/11, all packages were put on hold. Eventually, when the boards resumed, I was on a team set to deploy in the 9/11 efforts. Once I hit the third board and received news that I still didn't make it, the weirdest thing happened: I pressed on. They said no, but something inside me continued to hope.

My team was scheduled to leave in less than two weeks when, while at work, I received a call from the Military Personnel Flight. The Airman on the other end asked, "Is this Senior Airman Angela Blair?" I answered, "Yes." She then said, "Your crosstrain was approved." I remember vividly that my response was, "Huh?" Clearly, at that moment my faith was amiss, but with that simple call I was on my way to the next chapter in my life.

Everyone had told me, "Let it go. Angela, give up already, you are not getting this." Even someone in my leadership team told me that I was stupid to believe and that it would never happen for me. I swear, when you're working on attaining new levels, boy, does the devil show up. I was met with speed bump after speed bump after speed bump. If you notice, though, I said speed bump, not barrier, because my desire to retrain was so strong that nothing could get in my way.

PRINCIPLE 2: DO WHAT YOU BELIEVE IS RIGHT FOR YOU

In all honesty, this was probably my hardest lesson. Staying committed to something you feel is right for you can be challenging, especially when you're met with opposition from those closest to you. As I requested God to authenticate my life, I realized I won't always see eye-to-eye with everyone, but if it's right for me, GO FOR IT! In trusting God, though, my discernment grew stronger, allowing me to release what no longer served me and to nurture what energized me.

One area God was steering me toward was better health. Due to some health concerns I witnessed in the family, I knew if my daughters didn't have a better example of good health, things could turn out less than favorable for them. Without any real direction, I stopped eating red meat, then eventually all meat, finally canceling out animal products altogether and eating solely plant-based. This was before being vegan was fashionable, and let's just say my decision stirred up feelings from those close me.

Being vegan in a black family is a challenging matrix to move through. My food dishes were topics of discussion, and I was met with annoying jokes like, "There goes Angela eating her grass." Then there were the times I had to navigate through going out to eat with family, in which, most of the time, I didn't eat or I suffered through a lousy salad. I considered giving up my plant-based diet to return to eating meat, but I couldn't. The investment I was putting into my health held too much value to me, and to this day I am grateful for that choice. A quote of unconfirmed origin states, "So many people spend their health gaining wealth, and then have to spend their wealth to regain their health." I, however, was and am determined to buck that trend. Nowadays if I receive criticism for my nutritional choices it doesn't faze me. I'm proud to be thirty-seven, healthy, happy with my body, and grateful for the ability to keep up with my track-star daughter.

PRINCIPLE 3: IGNORE MORE, BECAUSE YOU CAN'T PLEASE EVERYONE

Have you seen the memes that read, "You're not an avocado, you can't please everyone"? Substitute your favorite food, i.e. chocolate, pizza, or coconut cake, in this catch phrase, but the fact is true. Some people will be with you for a lifetime, celebrating your high points and nursing you through the low ones. Other people are seasonal; they become envious of your highs and will celebrate the bad times that you endure. You deserve and should be experiencing high-vibe contact with people instead of harsh energy.

For years I had a "don't mess with her" reputation, which, unbeknownst to me, was due in part to who I was programmed to be, as well as from surrounding myself with the wrong individuals. My hard exterior was to mask the pain I concealed as I was being depleted from relationships with zero boundaries. But this quote from a sermon preached by Jamal Bryant changed my life: "If someone thinks that you're stuck up, it is their opinion, not a conviction. As a consequence it is not up to you to make them justify why they feel that way if you know that you're not." As my desire to live an authentic life grew, I used this quote as a reference point to develop a higher self-esteem.

The change was not about turning over a new leaf, but rather embracing the rebirth that was manifesting. Concerning yourself with outside influences only creates another hurdle for you to jump over. People will lie to you, gossip about you, and betray you, but don't let that be the end of your story. You can't worry about the unknown, dwell on your mistakes, or play the victim, because if you allow whatever people say about you to get to you, then you will go nowhere in life. Be neutral to outside opinions. If you are criticized, filter what is being said and don't take things personally. But, at the same time, you can't rely on others' praise to keep you afloat. We must be solid within ourselves, not teetering up or down based on others. Always remember, God has something beyond your imagination planned for you.

The most challenging event of my life was the loss of my grandmother in March 2015. She and I had a very special bond, definitely once in a lifetime. Toward the end of my marriage I began to harness a desire to live out my dreams, the deep down, real dreams that only I knew. During conversations on the phone or when I visited my grandmother she unknowingly affirmed them. "Look at my model; Precious, you belong on the cover of magazines," she would say. I never thought of myself as worthy. The negative commentary from people had me thinking I was inferior. Common. Basic. My grandmother's home going was difficult, and I thought I couldn't fulfill my dreams without her. Today, I know she is always with me and continues to coach me from heaven. I had a dream of writing a book, and I think ya'll see how that turned out. In the end, the opinion you have of yourself is the most valuable thing you will ever own.

PRINCIPLE 4: APOLOGIZE

Adulting is hard. We're not always on the side of right. We make mistakes. We're going to upset people. Although we are not responsible for people's reactions, we must take ownership of the words and actions that belong to us. People are more receptive than you think, especially when both parties come to the table ready to resolve conflict. An apology can do so much. It can mend relationships, heal a broken heart, and, most importantly, tell someone: I hear you, I see you, and you matter. My biggest problem growing up was that I was never taught how to manage my feelings or how to express myself in a way where others could better understand me. As a woman, being misunderstood is a very stifling feeling. I had to teach myself how to navigate through gossip, lies, and betrayals from people I held closest to me. Through those experiences I learned the art, as well as the value, of an apology.

There are times when an apology won't make a relationship move forward. Sometimes the healthy direction for a relationship is for it to end. Everyone has free will, meaning to accept or reject your apology is their choice. Case in point, I had what I thought to be a real friendship with someone. The two of us each hit a critical moment in our lives that required us to shift our focus and address those issues. Then, I began to notice a decline in responses to the text messages I sent to them. I reached out several times, asking if everything was good between us. I valued this person and wanted them to understand I was willing to address anything that may have offended them. After using several forms of communication, such as texts, calls, and emails, eventually I had to accept that this person had no interest in being friends. Truthfully, I had a vague idea of what had happened, but you can't let the insecurities of others stop you from living your life. Eventually I washed my hands of the situation, comfortable that I did everything within my power to fix what had broken.

Today I am very happy with the people in my life. I have also learned to accept that not everyone will apologize for what they did to you, and it is our responsibility to forgive them anyway. Truth is, our time on earth is just a dash. Use that time wisely on the ones you love, the people that bring you peace, that speak joy into your heart, and use the time to create something beyond your life that, years from now, will be seen and will inspire others to walk in their truth. Understand that if God removed someone from your life, He will replace that void with someone better suited for your life.

PRINCIPLE 5: COUNT YOUR BLESSINGS, THEN BLESS OTHERS

This principle is so obvious, but tends to fall on the wayside of life. There are so many things pulling us in different directions, such as work, kids, their sports, pets, the house, etc., but when you take the time to truly feel the power of gratitude, there is a miraculous improvement to your life. An attitude of gratitude can revert the negative, allowing positivity to change circumstances for the better. For instance, consider how different you feel when you are rushed from day-to-day activities versus when you sit down, bless your food, and feel how grateful you are to have that food. Knowing the food you're about to digest will be absorbed by your body and give you the fuel to move through the rest of the day feels different, right? I'm often guilty of not harnessing the feelings of gratitude, but when I do I feel better. My world is better. My girls perform better. My boyfriend is more loving. My finances multiply. All around, the things operating in my world are better.

When you honor God and feel the energy of being in awe of what He has done, you attract more to be grateful for. I can literally name numerous times when counting my blessings worked for me. One time in particular when I was thankful for my environment and trusting God, I received four job offers in one week. All of them put me in the six-figure lane, which was something I was praying for, so trust me when I say gratitude absolutely works.

The best part about being blessed is being able to bless someone else. Giving feels so much better than receiving, which is why I enjoy doing spontaneous things, such as giving money to a stranger, leaving a note on a receipt with a nice tip for wait staff, tithing, giving to charity, or, my favorite, helping single mothers get their footing. I have seen God's favor in my life, therefore it is my duty to pay it forward.

Over the years, I've made a series of decisions that did not match my heart, but God knows who we are and, just like any parent, He will arrange things to get me back on track. What I know for sure is that, when seemingly bad things transpire in life, their purpose is to get us to the next chapter. Some decisions are long overdue, but what will forever define our character is how we rise after falling.

FULFILLING YOUR DREAM WHILE LIVING YOUR PURPOSE

by Michelle Coleman

Few people truly know what they want to do for a living when they are young. Thankfully, God blessed me with that revelation when I was five. When my parents asked me what I wanted to be when I grew up, I told them a civil rights attorney (and a professional cheerleader). Wanting to be a lawyer at that age isn't unique. But unlike most kids, my goal of becoming an attorney never died. I owe that in part to my love of writing, debating, and solving problems. I also owe it to the encouragement of my loved ones and my decision to seize the various opportunities that have helped me on my journey. Most importantly, I have found that being an attorney is my purpose in life.

The road to fulfilling my purpose wasn't easy. I encountered a few potholes along the way. To date, my biggest obstacle was the very first step to becoming an attorney—getting into law school. To understand that terribly frustrating time, I must share a few details about myself.

You might expect that an aspiring attorney would have straight As throughout their educational career. Not me! While my hard work earned me the distinction of merit and the honor roll, there were periods where I felt my academic performance was less than stellar. Fortunately, my parents encouraged me to work hard and get a good education. They also taught me the importance of putting my trust in God and being a person of integrity. These values helped me in my pursuit of law school.

My law school preparation began in high school. I knew getting into college would require attaining good grades and participating in activities. Aside from that, though, I lacked a plan with courses of action (COAs) to achieve my goal. Everyone knows that a goal is pointless without COAs. Nonetheless, I had not developed a plan to help me execute step one—getting into law school. I no longer wanted to be a civil rights attorney, but I had no idea what type of law I did want to practice. I also had no clue which law school I wanted to attend. I am not saying that a high schooler should necessarily know their entire career path. I'm only saying that, if you have a goal, it is imperative to create a plan with COAs to help you attain the goal.

It wasn't until my sophomore year of high school when I attended the Oelschlager Summer Leadership Institute that the importance of time management and goal setting clicked. Prior to that, I never sat down to establish goals or action plans to accomplish them. I knew the outcome I wanted—to be an attorney—but didn't consider the journey to get there. The institute had a profound impact on me because it both taught me how to plan a career and improved my time management, critical thinking, and test-taking skills. With renewed vigor, I created a plan to pursue my goal.

My plan included several COAs. One COA included attending an undergraduate school in Ohio to capitalize on in-state tuition so that I could afford to attend a prestigious law school. I also decided to study business for a fallback career. Another COA included identifying a cabinet of people that I could consult. My cabinet included people who I could trust that knew my capabilities and weaknesses and were willing to provide me with sound guidance, encouragement, and constructive criticism. At the time, my cabinet included God, my parents, and my high school guidance counselor. Now my cabinet includes God, my husband, my parents, a mentor, and a colleague. Do you have a cabinet of people that you consult with on important life decisions? If not, create one. You should not pursue your goals alone.

A third COA included securing an internship with a local attorney. My friend's uncle practiced law and offered me an internship as a file clerk in high school. The internship introduced me to practicing law and courtroom etiquette. The attorney, a general practitioner, handled a multitude of issues. The internship made me realize that I did not want to be a general attorney and that I needed to do more research about the type of law I wanted to practice.

Additional COAs included attending Kent State University, getting involved in campus organizations and activities, finding internships, graduating with honors, and attending law school thereafter. I had no trouble with any of these COAs until it was time to apply for law school. In college I joined several organizations, interned with a judge and a government contractor, and graduated magna cum laude. The internship with the judge renewed my interest in trial practice. I fell in love with my work during my internship with the government contractor. I loved it so much I decided to attend George Washington University Law School so that I could pursue a career in government contract law. I felt on top of the world after crushing so many COAs—and then I took the Law School Admission Test (LSAT).

The LSAT was my first major obstacle. I am terrible at taking standardized tests. Despite knowing this about myself, I haphazardly took the LSAT, clearly underestimating the gravity of the exam. Before taking the exam, I convinced myself that I could adequately prepare myself while starting my senior year in college. Instead, I focused on other things, like working, graduating, and finding a job after college.

You are probably wondering why I let a life goal be put on the backburner. Perhaps I was too cocky. I assumed that studying a little and saying a prayer would be enough. Unfortunately, that plan resulted in a less than desirable LSAT score.

Not prioritizing my goal flopped. Have you ever looked up and realized that you failed to prioritize a goal? It happens, but you can overcome that setback by planning and recommitting yourself to the goal. It is discouraging when we aren't where we want to be, but the best thing to do is to learn from that setback and quickly move on.

This first disappointment was a good example of the mantra that "God helps those that help themselves." During this time my relationship with God was strained. I attended church when it was convenient and I rarely prayed because I could not be bothered to find the time for it. Yet there I was, asking God to help me get a good score without truly putting in the work. I treated God like a genie and it backfired.

After this disappointment, I regrouped and devised a plan to help me conquer the LSAT. I decided to take a year off between law school and college to work. I landed a government contract job in Virginia with the company I interned for during college. I also enrolled in Kaplan to help me prepare for the LSAT. I scheduled time outside of work and organizational commitments to study. I told everyone about my study schedule because I refused to compromise my study time.

My prayers asking God to reveal whether I should pursue law school were met with silence. I began to wonder if improving my LSAT score was the answer. Despite growing up in the church, my relationship with God was immature. I treated God like a genie by asking Him for the desires of my flesh. I wouldn't have recognized the answer anyway. I decided to press forward without an answer from God. It was no longer about attaining a goal, it was about proving that I could achieve the goal.

Enter obstacle two: applying for law school. Although my LSAT score improved, it did not carry the day. The three schools that I applied to rejected me. The law school admissions advisors told me I needed a higher LSAT score. It was a big blow to my ego because this time I had thoroughly prepared for the LSAT. I started to think that I wasn't smart enough to attend law school and began to consider other career options. I researched careers in contracts administration that would lead me to a position as the vice president of contracts—because surely my rejection by the law schools was a sign from God. After all, I had asked God to reveal whether law was the right career. I wouldn't struggle to get into law school if I was supposed to be an attorney, right? To make matters worse, everyone knew that I had applied to law school. It pained me to tell them I did not get in.

During my law school pursuit, I happened upon a quote by Beverly Sills that has since become my life's motto: "You may be disappointed if you fail, but you are doomed if you don't try." I am living proof of the truthfulness of this quote. If I had not persevered, I would not have fulfilled my purpose in life. Luckily, my parents and my future husband stepped in, offered me encouragement, and gave me the courage I needed to try again. When you fail, ask yourself if you are better off moving on. If you aren't, try again.

This story is a good example of how God moves on His own time, in His own way, and at the right time. Because of my difficulties in applying for law school and my resulting job while waiting, I became familiar with government contracts in a different way than most government contracts attorneys, which has paid off in dividends in my legal career. My experience served as a topic for my personal statement and I received tuition assistance while working there. Everything happened just as it should.

My rejections brought me back to the drawing board. I took another Kaplan course, withdrew from a few organizations, instituted a rigorous four-hours-a-day study schedule, and continued to pray for success on the exam and for a sign about my career. I ended up taking the LSAT at Kent State, which worked out because I would have the support of my family. A few days before the exam, though, my sister and I had an altercation. As a result, my father asked me to leave home. My dad has always been my cheerleader and he was aware of the importance of the LSAT. Nonetheless, he asked me to leave home with no place for me to stay two days before the test. My mom pleaded with me to stay and take the exam, but the damage was done. Lacking a place to stay, I drove all the way back to Virginia. Until this situation, I never knew that people that love and support you can stand in the way of your goals and dreams.

I decided to cancel the exam on the way home. I was too stubborn to drive back to Ohio and I thought the argument would compromise my ability to focus during the exam. Thankfully, my future husband convinced me to take the exam and drove me back to Ohio. After the exam, I felt at peace with my performance, despite the turmoil in my family.

After the exam, I knew if I didn't get into law school now, I never would. I continued to pray and ask God for a sign about applying to law school. I never thought my sign would come, until one day I randomly received a mailing from a diploma frame company selling George Washington Law School (GW Law) diploma frames—a frame that now secures my GW Law school diploma. I immediately knew that the random GW Law diploma mailing had to be a sign from God. Why else would I receive such a mailing? GW Law previously rejected me. Why would I even be on their mailing list? The sign renewed my spirit and boosted my confidence. Needless to say, GWU accepted me into their law program. Now I am a GWU law graduate practicing government contract law in the Washington, DC, area.

In hindsight, I understand that my struggle has made me a better attorney and a better person. Until this struggle, my life had been relatively easy. My struggle to get into law school was disappointing and it made me question my intelligence and self-worth. But it also humbled me and helped me learn how to handle disappointments. Life is full of disappointments. What matters is how you handle those disappointments. Sure, I sulk a little after a disappointment, but I don't let that stop me. I reflect on what went wrong and glean lessons from the situation that help me grow as a person and as a professional.

I don't consider a disappointment a failure if I've learned something from it. Merriam-Webster's online dictionary defines failure as "omission of occurrence or performance" and "lack of success" and defines success as a "degree or measure of succeeding" and a "favorable or desired outcome." Given the definitions of failure and success, I know that failure only occurs if I don't try or I don't learn from my disappointments. Thus, I rarely, if ever, fail.

Even after fulfilling my dream, I was still in search of God's purpose for my life. It wasn't until I started thinking about what part of my life to share in this book that my purpose came into focus. Even then, a friend had to tell me what had always been right before my eyes. I never thought that practicing law would be God's purpose for my life. I just thought that it was God's career choice for me. When I thought about God's purpose for my life, I thought that it had to be something grand, like becoming a missionary or a pastor. I never thought that God's purpose for my life could include something as simple as a full-time job. I always felt conflicted between my love for my career and the feeling that I needed to be doing more for God's kingdom. Now I know that I don't need to feel conflicted. I can share God's love with others simply by being kind and excelling at my job. It has given me great peace to know that I am right where God wants me to be. I still wonder if God wants me to do something that will have a greater impact on His kingdom. Nothing has been revealed to me at this time, but I welcome the challenge. Are you ready to accept the challenge?

TRUST THE PROCESS, GOD HAS A PLAN

by LaSheena Doxley

A person goes through so many ordeals and challenges in the process of living that it's difficult to place a finger on which circumstances lead to your evolving and which circumstances are just normal life challenges. Growing up in southeast Washington, DC, on Benning Road in the Eastgate Projects, as I did, life will truly challenge you. Chaos is the status quo, and morality is a concept that no one understands. Drugs, sex, violence, and lack of values are constants. On a daily basis you encounter multiple scenarios and interactions that can turn your life upside down. It's so chaotic and so barbaric that things like moral conflicts or ethical dilemmas are just a regular part of your day.

Perhaps you are facing daily challenges and struggles such as those I faced. If so, I want to share with you how—just like He did for me—God will cover you in the midst of it all and change your life around. God will lay out a series of subtle alterations in your life that will pick you up, turn you around, and pour out blessings that you could not at the time perceive. Mine came in a simple visit to my godmother's house, one that set off a series of life events that made me whole and brought power, purpose, and peace to my life. I will not pretend that the road was easy; however, in the midst of the tribulations, I began to know God for myself and, through knowing God, I became a wife, a mother, the holder of two degrees, and a testimony to the goodness of God.

If you asked anyone who knew me growing up, they wouldn't tell you of LaSheena Rice, who became LaSheena Doxley, they would tell you a story of "Bam Bam." A rough, tough, hyperactive child that would never sit down, would fight at the drop of a dime, and had little direction in life. To understand "Bam Bam," you first have to comprehend my background. My father has been incarcerated for most of my life; he went to jail for murder after defending my mother. He was a drug addict, a thief, and a convicted criminal even before his sentence for the murder charges. He is the person that introduced my mother to drugs. Those drugs are what brought chaos and pain into my mother's life. She became an addict at a very young age and, because of her addiction, she lost everything, including her children. She would run the streets all night, meeting man after man, having no regard for her motherly responsibilities. Because of her actions, I had to live with my late grandmother, my pride and joy, Ms. Minnie Mae Rice. She took me in as well as my younger sister and brother. The big heart that allowed my grandmother to take me in also had her take in my uncles and my mother as well. Imagine growing up with your mother in the same house, but you don't see her as a mother. She was there physically, but she never took on the responsibility of a mother; she didn't nurture, care for, or provide for us. I would go weeks without seeing her and would constantly worry over whether or not she was okay. It was devastating.

Our daily lives consisted of loss and pain; my mother and her siblings were all alcoholics and drug addicts that fought both outsiders and each other nearly every weekend. My childhood was filled with family gatherings that were marred with violence. It was difficult for me, a child who yearned for family, to have no peace. I grew up a sad child, desiring family, wanting structure within my family, and wishing for family togetherness. But these life challenges were God molding me, sculpting me to be a person that would one day be in a position to help other families. Although I did not realize it until later in life, my challenging childhood is where I gained my passion for being a family advocate and cultivated a desire to impact families in a positive manner, where I established my desire to take chaos and bring about order.

Even with that desire, however, the pain did not cease, the violence continued, and it kept me in a constant state of sadness and panic. But little did I know that my godmother, Mrs. Theresa Reed, would extend an olive branch to me that would change the entire trajectory of my life. She reached out to my grandmother one day and offered for me to come to San Diego to visit for a summer. It was the summer of 1993 when I made my trip to San Diego, California; this visit changed my entire life. My visit for a summer would become a permanent place of residence and my new home.

My San Diego years can be considered some of the best and worst times of my life. It was there where my godmother began to instill in me the value of getting to know God for myself. She also instilled in me the confidence to be myself and be who I was always meant to be. I can vividly remember her constantly telling me that one day I would become a household name. It seemed like not one day went by without her saying in her loud, boisterous voice, "LaSheena, one day your name will be a household name," or "You are gonna have a household name!" I didn't realize it at the time, but this mantra became a sense of identity for me. Her words gave me identity and purpose—but they would also become the source of my greatest fears and agony. What happens to a person who believes they will be a household name when life doesn't go as planned? Are you a failure if you reach twenty-one years of age and you are not yet a household name? Are you a failure if you reach twenty-five and everyone in the world does not know your name? Are you an absolute disaster if you reach the age of thirty and find that not only are you still not a household name, but, to top it off, you are also lost, and have no direction or purpose in life? These were the questions I faced throughout my life and which often left me in my deepest states of depression and self-doubt. I would reach these milestone birthdays, and yet I felt at each of those moments like my life had no merit and that I had accomplished nothing in my days on earth.

Then, my godmother, who was my only confidant, was violently taken from me, as she was murdered by her husband in February of 2006. So I had no one that I could trust with my feelings, who understood my pain, or with whom I could express my insecurities. There was no peace in my life and I had no direction or path to find it. It was a challenge to try to live with a purpose when I could not find a purpose. I had no foundation, my greatest advocate was taken from me, and, in my mind, to that point in my life I had not achieved anything.

Life is not linear, where one thing lines up after another. Life is random and spontaneous. I was in my late twenties, married, with four children, and I had tried multiple online colleges hoping to find direction and purpose. Due to numerous factors, however, these endeavors failed and all I was left with was growing debt, a frustrated husband, and a greater sense of failure than ever before. I began to think I would never find purpose; however, in my life of no purpose, my desire to help others and bring order to chaos sent me in a new direction. God led me to accept my nephew into my home when he was just six years old. Even though I was already a mother of four, I brought in a fifth child. God gave me a sense to help those in need, and the child in need that I helped actually wound up helping me find my purpose in life. My nephew was diagnosed with a clinical problem and was given counseling services. Through a conversation with his counselor, I was informed of a dual licensure program at a university forty minutes from my home that offered the only program in marriage and family therapy and counseling in my state. The glory of God is shown right there; He tailored a situation for me, one that only I could solve, which led me to my future institution of higher learning.

From that conversation with my nephew's counselor, I was led to my new chapter in life. I was thirty-two years old with no purpose, and through a good deed, bringing my nephew into our already crowded home, God opened up a door for me that led me to where I am at this very moment. After speaking with my nephew's counselor, I started doing research on the University of Akron and their program, the only one within the state of Ohio. And remember my failures, the ones from taking the online courses where I did not succeed? Well, this program was within driving distance of my home, and I was able to travel and take the courses in a classroom setting, which was more conducive to my learning style. I had to take a second and marvel at how God worked, unraveling the chaos in my life and laying out a path to a blessing in a way that only He can.

The path was laid out, but taking the steps and going through the process were not easy. Even following the plan God had for me was difficult. I had to step out of my comfort zone as a wife and become a college student all over again, after ten years, five children, and thousands of miles since my last experience at a university. I had to embark on a journey into the unknown, leaving my husband to be the provider of the house, the man of the house, leaving him with his roles and duties and adding all of mine onto his plate. I stepped out, trusting that God would keep my family, as I had to mother from a distance at best for the next three years. Trust me, those three years were just as challenging as the thirty-two prior to that, maybe even more so. While I was finally doing something to better myself, the dynamics in my household were turbulent. Yet, there I was, a nontraditional student who was able to graduate with a master of arts degree, a dual licensure in marriage and family counseling and in therapy. The road was hard, but I will never forget the joy my husband and children had watching me walk across the stage or the huge congratulations that I received upon completion of my journey. The reward was definitely worth all the pain. God restored my sense of purpose and the joy in my life. God took all of my misfortunes, doubts, and fears and turned them into a success story.

Even in that success, there are still challenges. God allows your faith to be tested. What I didn't mention earlier is that, upon graduation, you still have to take a licensure exam. The first time I took my licensure exam, I failed by one point. That experience brought me to my knees, because it was in that moment that I realized that God had opened a door for me to escape my current situation, a problem I hadn't recognized I had. I realized that my home, my husband, and my children were out of order and our lives were chaotic. Failing my licensure exam brought Mom back home and into their lives. We spent a summer getting to know each other all over again. I was able to refocus spiritually, mentally, and physically. My household had peace again, my kids had their mother back, my husband had his wife back, and order was restored in our home. That summer was one of the most joyous of my life because I reconnected with them and with God on a daily basis.

Ahead of me, I still had one milestone left to reach, and that was passing my licensure exam. I studied diligently while trying to maintain balance in my home. In the days leading up to my exam, I experienced fear, anxiety, and self-doubt, wondering if I'd once again be close to my goal but miss my certification by one point. Just to show that God was not through with me yet, by His grace my hard work paid off and I passed my exam the second time around to become a board-certified, licensed professional counselor.

We all have to remember that there is something on the inside of us, even in the face of tragedy, depression, and failure, that God implanted in us a long time ago and that we have to bring out. Through Him and through our faith we can make it to our winning season. We just have to trust Him and do the work ourselves, giving Him glory and honor every step of the way. I did not realize during my troubles that God did not create me to worry or fear. All I need to do is trust in Him and watch Him work wonders in my life; trusting God begins with me walking by faith and not by sight (2 Corinthians 5:7). My story is a testimony to all those who feel like they have not achieved what they want to with their life. God says it's not over, your life's not over, and He is not through with you yet. Sometimes your darkest hour is just a new beginning and a sign of brighter days. This testimony is made to share with you that it is not your timeline, or your script, it's God's. He has the final say with your life, and if you trust in Him and believe in Him, He will work wonders in your life and set you on a path to purpose and peace. Look at this screenshot into my life: I am here to proclaim that He is not through with me yet; instead He is setting me on a path to fulfill His destiny and purpose in my life. This is just stage one of LaSheena Renee Doxley becoming a household name. I have found peace in trusting the process through my faith in God.

A MOTHER'S LOVE

by Jenell Brown

When did this all start? You know, I get that question all the time. How did you know that something was not right, that something was wrong with him? Wrong? I hate the word wrong and its definition when it's linked to describing my son. Nothing is wrong with him, he's just a typical seven-year-old boy, one with various challenges that range from being overly aggressive to super emotional, varying depending on the situation. I have to put that lightly because, as a mother, I've had no choice but to learn to protect and advocate for my child for the last three years in ways I would have never imagined.

When William was about a year and a half old I started watching him closely; I watched his ways, I followed his patterns, and I paid close attention to his moods and behaviors. That was when he started to do something that is referred to as "eloping." If I wasn't paying attention, William would go off with strangers or wander off from wherever we were without a moment's notice. Petrifying, right? Yes, more than petrifying, talk about your heart skipping a beat when you can't find your child and he's only a toddler. He was very active, hard to keep calm or still for a normal period of time. Most people would say that that sounds like a normal kid, but there was more to his actions. He was a bit different. Different from my first son, who was almost four years old when I started noticing these behaviors in William.

William is my second son and was born during an ugly divorce between his father and I. He was not born due to my wanting a second child; he just happened while I was going through a failed marriage and hurt from my ex-husband's cheating habits. I felt a sense of guilt for even wanting to go through with my pregnancy, knowing that we were not going to be together to raise our second child. Nonetheless, I went through the pregnancy full-term and delivered William in Austin, Texas, through cesarean section due to labor complications. He was a beautiful, dark-brown-haired baby boy, pale as can be, with such an innocent look to him. His tiny fingers were so fragile and soft, and in his quiet moments his little pink lips would clasp together with a slight smile. He was named William after my mother, father, and late grandmother, and his big brown eyes reminded me of my mother. He was a special child even before I knew how special he was going to be. My family and friends were instantly drawn to him once he was home from the hospital. I had the best support system that any single mother could desire. I remember my great aunt would come to pick up my oldest son every day just to give me time with William.

William's father was absent during the early months of his life. I was somewhat okay with that until I realized I needed some sort of relief, or just time to rest and heal from the pregnancy. I initially had a good routine with raising the boys alone, but I had limited time from trying my hardest to devote myself to being a good mother to two needy boys. It was difficult to say the least, because William called for more of my attention. I was constantly circling back to his every move or following directly behind him, because he was a busy baby. Busy is the best way to describe a toddler who was as active as a squirrel searching every crevice for food. William would be at the top of the couch, on the kitchen counter, in the cabinets, or even in the dryer if the door was left open to the garage. William's father became more present in his life once he was about a year old. He would take the boys for short visits and overnight stays. We were not the best at co-parenting, due to the circumstances of our failed relationship, but we did what we could.

As time went by, William's behavior became more evident to the people around me. People questioned his habits and behavior and even gave him the nickname of "Action William." My life was busy; I tried to juggle being a mother, working, having a social life, and even dating while I was parenting a challenging child. It was hard! Hard and complicated.

During the summer of 2012, I let my guard down and released my fear of being away from the boys, allowing them to go away to Minnesota with their father for about a month. This was the only time William had been away from me for such a long amount of time and I worried furiously. I wondered if his father was going to pay close attention to him like I did, if William was going to wander off, if his father's family would care for him or love him like I did. So many thoughts ran through my head. I constantly called to check in on them, to see if everything was okay. When the boys returned at the end of July, I asked their father several questions about how they did—but, like usual, he refused to answer my questions or responded with short, nonchalant answers in order to get me to stop asking concerning questions.

It took a bit to transition William back into my home lifestyle. William had become a bit aggressive and extremely defiant. The time-outs and naptime punishments just didn't seem to work anymore for him. Thankfully, my then-boyfriend and I were steady and rooming together, so it helped, having a male figure to help with the discipline side. It worked a little. It was more challenging because William was enrolled in daycare. I would get nonstop calls about his behavior, that William had hit another kid, or that the staff had found William on the other side of the center. It was hard to keep a level head while I was working full-time, because I never knew what the next call would be.

To help reduce the amount of time William was in day-care, I enrolled him into an early public school pre-k program. I somehow thought that the change of environment would alleviate certain behavioral issues—but instead they increased. I remember receiving a call from William's teacher, saying she found William over by the school buses, away from where his normal pickup was located. I was extremely flustered. How did he get way over there? Was no one paying attention? The teacher and I started to establish a good relationship where she was one hundred percent on board with assisting with his moods and behaviors. My only outlet and resource at the time was his teacher, so I took advantage of her goodwill and support to help me with my son.

William successfully went through his first year of public school. During that year, my now-husband was transferred overseas to a location where the boys and I were not able to go, so we stayed in Texas with my mother and father. It worked out well, because I had an extra set of adults to help me with the boys. After spending a year away from the family, my husband received official orders relocating us to Las Vegas. I was excited but sad, because I knew I would be leaving behind my strong village of support who had helped me with William for the last four years.

Once we moved to Las Vegas, William's behaviors became more extreme. We were settling in to our new home and I was starting a job that was about an hour away. After the first week at my new job, I got a call from my husband's First Sergeant saying that he had been trying to locate my husband and me, as he had received a call from Security Forces that they had custody of my son with obsessive compulsive disorder (OCD). I frowned. In my mind, I was thinking, OCD? Who is he talking about? At that time, William had not been diagnosed or been seen by a doctor. The First Sergeant continued talking and describing what actually happened, and immediately tears began to roll down my face. He was talking about William. William had wandered off from my home while under the care of a family member and was found about half a mile away from the house. He had found his way to the base youth center. The day prior to the incident I had enrolled two of my children into the youth center, as William was too young at the time to be able to go, and he was with me when I enrolled the other two. Needless to say, I was too anxious to allow the First Sergeant to finish the conversation before I informed my new boss that I had to leave because my son had gotten out of my house. Keep in mind we were in the middle of a Las Vegas summer, where temperatures can range from 115–125 degrees Fahrenheit. I couldn't even think straight on the way home. What if he got dehydrated? What if a vicious dog was out and attacked William? How would I be able to process losing my son to his eloping behaviors?

I prayed on that hour-long drive home and just thanked God continuously for the safety and protection of my son. God was my only saving grace and outlet during those moments. I felt like no one would ever understand what it feels like to experience this type of scare. By that time William had eloped multiple times in his life, and never once did the feeling get easier when he was found safely. I never felt at ease. His behaviors were so unpredictable that I could never let my mind rest. I would speak to William one-on-one and ask what was going through his head and why he left. Of course, being a young kid, he would never provide any real answers; he would normally just reply by saying his brain told him to do it.

School was about to start and I feared entering into yet another school year in a different location. To make things easier on my family, the kids attended school on base. During the first week of school the calls started. This time, the calls included behaviors where William was violent with the teacher, where the teacher had to evacuate the class due to him destroying the teacher's property, or where he would not come back into the class after recess. I was tired; well, I had been tired since his first year at school. So I would spank William, put him in time-out, make him go to bed early, everything. The calls continued. By the fourth week of school, the principle suspended him and stated he could not return until I had a meeting with the administration team. I met with the team and they described William as if he were a demon. They said that he would be moved to a different classroom, which might possibly help. Unfortunately, it didn't.

On William's fifth birthday I got a call that I needed to pick him up, that he was suspended again. I tried to ask the details behind what was going on, but they would not fill me in. It took me an hour to get to William's school. During that hour I had received two additional calls to see if I was on my way. No peace.

Being new to the school district, I didn't know what resources were available for my child, and I was frustrated that the school was not supportive at all. I needed the school to help me in my transition, but they continuously sent William home for his behavioral issues rather than provide alternative solutions. I asked the principal tons of questions about options or programs to help keep William in school, but I received no help or viable options. Each time William was suspended, I had to take those days off work, because there was no care set up to watch him during the day. I burned through my work leave and I literally was taking time off without leave. Something had to give. I needed help and I needed it quick.

Whenever William was able to return to school, he was quickly suspended again for destruction of property and being aggressive. William's behaviors started to pour into our home life, too, and it was hard for me to control him in the house with our other children present. My other children became victims to his aggression. I needed to get William help, so I researched a local treatment facility and called to request their assistance. They told me to bring William in to be assessed. I brought William in, and that very day they admitted him into their acute care program for approximately nine days. It was the first time I had ever reached out medically to figure out what was going on with my son.

During his stay in the facility, William was diagnosed as pediatric bipolar, which was later changed to disruptive mood deregulation disorder (DMDD) and attention-deficit hyperactivity disorder (ADHD). They also prescribed him his first medications to help control or decrease the amount of aggressive behaviors. Once William was discharged, he returned back to school. I went back again and asked the school for support, and they put William on a behavior plan. It was explained to me that this plan would be used in the event of behavioral incidents to try to redirect him. They also stated that the calls to come get him would be less due to this plan. That's all I needed; I wanted the calls to stop! I wanted to stop worrying at work about when the next call would come.

Fortunately, all of William's care was paid for through my husband's military benefits. A case manager through our insurance contacted me one day, and to this day I'm not sure what made her call that day, but the timing was right. I was actually on my way to the school to get William because he had charged after the teacher with scissors. The case manager listened to my tears of frustration, my plea for help. I told her how I'd tried researching help around the Las Vegas area, but all the therapists or psychologists refused to see him because he was so young. I told her how the only help I'd received was the outpatient support from the treatment facility. She gave me a list of resources that ranged from local support groups to a list of doctors to contact that she was sure would see him. She also told me that if things got worse I should just take William to the emergency room.

After his first stay in treatment, William's language was a little more creative. He began to use that language at school and started using it at home during his moments. For the next year, William was in and out of the acute treatment center about seven times, ranging from a week to two weeks each time. His medication changed over twenty times, but still nothing was helping to manage his behaviors. The last straw came when William had been suspended from school and decided he was going to run away from home. When I located him, I took him to the military emergency room. That day, I found out that the base had finally gotten a developmental-behavioral doctor, who came to see William while in the ER. He explained to me the severity of William's case and recommended residential treatment. The thought hurt my heart because I knew it meant William would be away for some time. The military approved the treatment and within months William was admitted into a residential treatment facility in Texas. It was a long six and a half months away from my son. There were nights I cried myself to sleep, wondering if I had made the right decision.

But I noticed a sense of peace in my home, a relief from the chaos and constant physical strain I was going through to help my son. I used this time to research, read, and meet with my own therapist to get me through. I also had our bishop come in to bless our home and pray with my family to make sure we were going to make it through. I realized that this may not be the way I ever imagined parenting, but I do it because I love my son. I learned different ways to parent a challenging child and how to be gentle and sensitive to his needs. I know this journey is not over and we still have a long road ahead of us, but with God, my support system, my therapist as well as William's therapist, the support of my case manager, and the military, we will continue to manage William's behaviors and will go through in the future.

PAIN GUARANTEES WE LACK NOTHING AND LIVE IN ABUNDANCE

by Resealia McKinney

I am a believer in a God who loves me in such an intimate way, it overwhelms me at times. I am a wife to my husband of fourteen years who too loves me in ways I don't always deserve or reciprocate, yet he loves me still. I am a counselor by profession, which comes as no surprise to those who know me. My very nature is to help, encourage, and empathize with others. Since I was a little girl, I dreamt of having the perfect family: a loving husband and three or four kids. I often envisioned my husband and I raising our children as we blended our values, our upbringings, and, most importantly, the truths we have gleaned through the Word of God and our personal relationships with Him.

Early on in our marriage, my husband and I discussed not having children too soon, as we wanted time to learn one another, travel, and enjoy each other. We felt we needed to be solid in our marriage before children came along. We agreed we would know when the time was right to start building our family. It was three and a half years into our marriage before we decided we were ready to get pregnant. We were confident we would soon be sharing exciting news with family and close friends, but as month after month passed, our excitement began to wane. I can recall often thinking, "This is the month. I'm pregnant!" I spent lots of money on pregnancy tests only for them to consistently show I wasn't pregnant. I remember crying at times when my menstrual would come, especially after I talked myself into believing I was pregnant.

We decided it was time to seek help. We went to doctors who termed our diagnosis as "unexplained infertility." There wasn't an explanation for why we were not conceiving. Neither clinging to prophecies spoken over us that we would get pregnant nor praying faith-filled prayers to a God we knew answered prayer seemed to help. Our faith-filled prayers were losing their zeal. Doubt began to set in. We began to wonder if our prayers would ever be answered. We began to despair and lose hope. We wanted so desperately to be parents. I had grown weary in praying and depended heavily on the prayers of others, partly because I was tired of being let down after getting my hopes up yet again. We gave it to God. We realized we did not have any control over the situation. We were doing what we knew to do, but we were not getting any results. For three years, we prayed and prayed. We found books to encourage our faith, such as *Supernatural Childbirth* by Jackie Mize. The author was told she would never have children; however, she decided to stand on the word of God and was blessed as a result with four children. We prayed the prayers included in this book over my womb, believing God would bless us, too.

In 2008, our lives changed. My church customarily does a seven-day consecration at the start of each new year. I had not eaten in three days and had only drunk water. By the third day, I became extremely nauseous. I could barely stand. My first thought was that it was the result of not eating. Pregnancy, bizarrely enough, was not my initial thought. Nevertheless, I decided it would not hurt to take a test. To my amazement, we were pregnant! I was overjoyed and so thankful God had answered our prayers. Initially, my pregnancy went very smoothly. No morning sickness, just a substantially larger appetite. I could not complain at all, compared to some of the horror stories I had heard relating to pregnancy.

We anticipated a healthy pregnancy and hoped for a healthy baby girl. Although the sex of our baby could not yet be determined, I always referred to her as a baby girl. We decided to name her Reese Madison. At nineteen weeks, though, pregnancy as I knew it changed. I noticed something unusual. In a panic, I called my doctor to notify them I was leaking fluid. I was assured during my visit that all was well, but to notify them if the issue continued. They wanted to confirm it was not amniotic fluid leaking. This alarmed me, as I knew amniotic fluid was essential for my baby's survival. I knew it provided the necessary nutrients my baby needed.

Within a couple of weeks, I felt the leak again. I immediately recalled my doctor's concern and prayed it was not amniotic fluid. Because it was after hours, my husband and I headed to the emergency room. The doctor confirmed it was undeniably amniotic fluid leaking and termed it "premature rupture of membranes." My water had begun to break early. At a follow-up visit, it was suggested we see a specialist. When we did, the specialist emphatically stated with no emotion that our baby would not survive, as there was very little amniotic fluid left. He encouraged us to abort the pregnancy and wanted us to make a decision right then. Tears streamed down our faces as we called our family and friends to pray. That was all we knew to do. My heart was breaking. I was in disbelief this was actually happening. Yet we left the specialist's office believing God would grant us a miracle. This was the child we prayed for; God *had* to move on our behalf.

One doctor supported our decision not to abort and recommended I be admitted into the hospital until I delivered. To me, this seemed to be the better option, where I could be consistently monitored, as I was already on bedrest. We entered into the hospital at close to twenty-three weeks pregnant, praying to get to at least thirty weeks, as the doctor had shared with us that this increased the chances of our baby's survival. Although hearing my baby's heartbeat warmed my heart, the whole experience, as I was poked and prodded by nurses several times a day, felt unreal.

One evening in the hospital, I discovered a greenish substance leaking and I called for a nurse. I was told they would continue to monitor me and not to worry. A few days passed. I was close to twenty-five weeks when I saw the substance again after being awakened to use the restroom in the wee hours of the morning. I again called for a nurse. This nurse's reaction to the news was much different. She said it could be signs of my baby having a bowel movement, which could be poisonous to us both. She then stated what I did not want to hear: we needed to deliver our baby . . . now! I was exactly twenty-five weeks. Before I could utter a word, the nurse hurried out to alert others that I needed to be prepped for a C-section. Thank God my husband was there with me. Things were happening so fast. I was whisked off to get an epidural as my husband followed close behind. When we arrived, he was asked to wait in another room. Our eyes connected as we silently prayed again for a miracle.

I can recall hearing the doctor exclaim our baby was indeed a girl and seeing tears of joy streaming down my husband's face. Reese Madison was here—but our birth story was anything but typical. We didn't hear the cries of our newborn, didn't get to hold or kiss our baby. We weren't able to see her as she was hastily taken to get medical care in the neonatal intensive care unit (NICU). I had so many questions. Why was this happening? What were they doing to her? Was she going to survive? I could not process it all. She was born prematurely, so I didn't know what to expect, as she only weighed in at 1.2 pounds. I asked some of these questions to family members, but based on their elusive responses, I could tell the prognosis was not favorable. After what seemed like forever, doctors finally came in to speak to me. I was told very little oxygen had gotten to our Reese Madison's brain. Yet, I still had hope. I still believed in a miracle. God was the giver of life! Surely our baby girl was supposed to be here.

The next day, one of Reese Madison's lungs collapsed. They had to resuscitate her, which doctors said caused trauma to her tiny body. We were asked to sign paperwork releasing them from performing that procedure again. I hesitated to sign. "God, please move on our behalf," I prayed over and over. My husband looked me in the eyes and said, "Baby, she does not have enough oxygen. Without oxygen, she can't survive." The reality of what was happening began to sink in. Our baby, who we had prayed for, for so long and so desperately, was going to die. We couldn't stop it from happening. We as her parents were supposed to protect her, but her life was slipping away from us with each passing moment.

I held her as long as I could. She was absolutely perfect. She looked up at me as if she knew I was there with her. The nurse validated this truth. She reassured me that we made the best decision for our child and that good parents make decisions, even if difficult, to do what is best for their children. She went on to say that Reese Madison knew we were there with her as she fought for her life and for every breath she took. I didn't want to leave her side; however, my health became a concern, as I had a high fever and was experiencing chills, so much so I was literally shaking. I was urged to rest.

We were awakened by a nurse coming into our room the next morning, asking us to get down to the NICU immediately. I was taken down in a wheelchair with my husband following close behind. As soon as we arrived, Reese Madison was placed in my arms as she took her last breath. What we feared most was happening. After two short days on earth, our baby girl died. We let out the most gut-wrenching sobs as we watched her die. They gave us as much time as we desired to hold her. Again, I didn't want to let go. She was so perfect and so beautiful. I rubbed her silky, straight black hair. I held on tightly as my dreams of being a mother seemed to die along with her. Would we still be considered parents? Would she be remembered? How could I leave this hospital empty-handed? But I didn't have a choice. My baby had died and we were left to put the pieces of our lives back together again.

My hope seemed in vain. My dream shattered. My home empty. Silence and sobs echoed through our home. I was an emotional wreck. I felt like my body had failed me. I wasn't able to carry my baby full-term. I felt like God had failed me. Our prayers weren't answered. We didn't have an explanation as to why my water broke early. We just knew our baby girl was no longer here. I felt like I had been stabbed in the pit of my stomach, my breath taken away with each memory of Reese Madison.

The years following the death of our daughter were painful to bear. Then, in 2010, two years after losing our daughter, we learned my husband had cancer. He would be diagnosed with it again in 2012 and 2016. We couldn't seem to get a break from bad news and heartache. I wasn't sure if we could bear it all, but our faith in Jesus kept us.

Everyone is given a measure of faith. God knows how much faith each of us needs to sustain us. He knows us and how much we can endure. He walked the road of suffering before us. Nothing catches Him by surprise. My faith was attacked during those difficult times and I doubted God. I wavered in my confidence of His goodness. I felt abandoned by Him. It seemed the more I prayed, the more He was silent. As I clung to Jesus and began to study the Word of God, though, I realized no one is exempt from suffering. The Bible promises we will all experience trials. The Bible also encourages us to give thanks in all things, as this is the will of God for our lives (1 Thessalonians 5:18). This sounds contradictory, doesn't it? I sure thought so. How can I give thanks after my daughter died or after my husband battled cancer, not once or twice, but three times? But scripture does not tell us to give thanks *for* everything, but *in* everything. Why? Because our trials perfect us. They bring purpose to our lives and a compassion for others we never knew existed. Most importantly, they guarantee we lack nothing (James 1:3–4).

Prior to our suffering, I had a false sense of assurance that everything in life would be easy. Don't be mistaken, I didn't grow up spoiled rotten. Nevertheless, I was able to accomplish most things I set out to do with ease. I thought if I said a prayer, like making wishes to a genie, I would have whatever I prayed for. But through my suffering I learned this is not how God operates. First and foremost, He cares more about us becoming more like Him than anything—more than giving us the desires of our hearts, more than fulfilling our dreams, more than answering our prayers. His ultimate desire is for us to be more like Him.

My life's purpose is to connect women to this truth. To introduce them to a God who loves them immensely and who wants their love in return. To showcase a personal relationship so intimate it overshadows every other desire. To encourage women to believe, in spite of their pain, that God is amazing. He does not allow pain to destroy us. Instead He uses it to bless us. If we could, we would all shield ourselves from pain. No one wants to experience it. Jesus didn't want to, yet He knew what God the Father desired for Him was the best plan. Despite pain and sorrow, He followed the plan of the One who mattered most. As should we. My life's work is to inspire women to guard their hearts against discontentment and bitterness. Use your pain to draw closer to Him.

My story has not changed. Perhaps yours has not either. Although we haven't been blessed with more children, nor has my husband received complete healing from cancer, I choose to believe God's love for me is unquestionable. I trust His plan for my husband and I to become parents. I believe my husband will be healed. I also still believe, no matter what, that He is good. I hope you can believe that too.

WHERE IS GOD?
A JOURNEY
OF BROKENNESS
AFTER LOSS

by Brittany Hogan

"Where is God? Why would he allow such heartbreaking circumstances to happen to His children?" When life comes crashing in, these are the first thoughts that enter most of our minds.

These are questions my husband and I asked ourselves during two consecutive summers as we lost our first two children to premature birth. You see, my husband and I, like most newly married couples, were excited to start a family. We had both found jobs in our respective fields, him in marketing and me in physical therapy—we were on our way. We had been married for two years and felt God nudging us to begin trying to conceive sooner than we had planned. Although hesitant, we couldn't deny the assurance of the direction we were getting, and by December of 2014 we had scheduled our first visit to the doctor to gain their insight. Due to a previous health scan revealing a diagnosis of polycystic ovarian syndrome (PCOS), I knew I would need mild assistance to get pregnant, but there were no concerns otherwise. We were excited and ready to begin the process.

After only two short months we were pregnant, and ecstatic to say the least. God had answered our prayer to conceive, and every ultrasound displayed the healthy baby we couldn't wait to hold in just nine months. Our pregnancy was filled with exciting pregnancy announcements and even more exciting gender reveal parties that divulged our big secret—we would welcome our first daughter to the world on Nov 22, 2015. What a blessing! I would get the mini-me I've always desired.

Every aspect of this pregnancy was perfect until July 3, 2015. I remember it so well because we were about to cross the five month mark and I was in full planning mode, preparing our home and schedules for our baby, who we had recently named Niya Alise. That morning I began to have unusual symptoms of discharge and mild cramps. I called the on-call doctor, since it was the weekend, and in an encouraging tone he instructed me to simply follow up with our doctor on Monday. I was mildly concerned, but tried to accept the doctor's encouragement—until the next night I began to experience what I now know to have been contractions while watching TV with my husband and sister. This debilitating pain that wrapped around my entire waist was very concerning, but because of the doctor's tone the day before, I attempted to just take two Tylenol pills to address it, even though my husband and sister both wanted me to call the doctor. We agreed that if the pain did not subside in one hour after the Tylenol, I would call. One hour passed and the contractions were just as intense, if not more so.

I called the doctor and was fortunately transferred to the same one from the previous night. In the middle of me explaining my symptoms, he interrupted me by saying, "Mrs. Hogan! Mrs. Hogan! I want you to come to Labor and Delivery immediately." We packed up immediately and drove to the hospital. When we finally made it, the nurse checked my cervix and concluded that the contractions I felt were probably only Braxton Hicks, assured me I would be fine, and prepared to discharge me. I began to bleed shortly after she left the room and my husband ran to inform her. She didn't budge. She only assured him that it was normal. We would learn later that the amount of bleeding I was experiencing was far from normal. But again, in an endeavor to trust our healthcare providers in light of our amateur understanding of the pregnancy journey, we left the hospital with a plan to follow up with my doctor the next morning.

Unfortunately, the pain and bleeding from the night continued and increased into the next morning. I attempted to call my doctor at eight o'clock sharp but was met with a voicemail. After getting this message four or five times, I selected the choice to be connected to the on-call physician via the operator. When the operator answered, she informed me that she could not connect me to an on-call physician because according to her records my doctor was in the office. So there I was, bleeding and contracting, with no direction of what to do next.

Desiring to find peace during this time, I began to pray and confess the Word of God over my baby in between calling family and friends. I knew God had instructed us to begin trying to conceive. I was not going to allow the enemy to steal what God had blessed us with. I prayed and believed that everything would be fine even in the midst of continued bleeding and pain.

After a couple of hours passed with no answers or assistance, a friend offered to take me to the hospital. When we arrived we were met with a locked door before and after the lunch hour. Completely irritated at the lack of care, my husband arrived and began searching for someone to see me until finally he was instructed to take me to Labor and Delivery. "Thank you, God!" I thought. Answered prayer. Surely our baby would be just fine. We had prayed and we were trusting that, just like many times before, God would blow our minds with an amazing blessing. When we arrived, however, we were met with a sweet nurse and later a doctor who would deliver the worst news we had ever heard—I was already three centimeters dilated and I would inevitably go into labor.

What? This is not how this was supposed to end. We had prayed. I was sure God would rescue us. Those words would begin the most devastating season of our lives. Although the doctors did as much as they could to lessen the contractions, I gave birth to Niya at 1:46 a.m. the next morning at exactly twenty weeks and two days. She lived a short, sweet six minutes before passing away in my arms.

The heartbreak of birthing a child you know will not make it seems almost unbearable. Why had God forsaken us?

We questioned everything. Should we have ignored the doctor and come sooner? Did we not pray the right things? Had we disobeyed God in some way that was causing this lack of His goodness? I searched my journals, the Bible, questioned even God's love for us. How could He allow something so horrible for someone He loves? Have you asked these questions after experiencing a loss?

My natural response was to push through. I'm an oldest child and a natural leader. Taking the punches in stride is what I do. But this punch was too difficult to bear. The day after I came home I remember waking up crying. The devastation seemed fresh each day I woke. I wanted to do what I was used to doing and simply push through, but this level of pain was more than I could handle. I knew that running to God in this was the right thing to do, but I couldn't bear it. He had betrayed me, so I felt. Although I wasn't the nicest to Him, I learned that this is exactly what He wanted me to do. Run to Him. As we questioned, screamed, and cried, He spoke a truth in our hearts that we've never forgotten: "Trust requires a great degree of uncertainty." Although He wasn't giving us answers, He asked us to trust His goodness and heart for us, the same way we trust that of our earthly fathers. Even though it didn't seem like it, He was hurting with us and desiring we allow Him to piece our hearts back together.

Following the death of our daughter Niya, God used so many people, His Word, and even books to help us pick up the pieces and attempt to try again. Although we hoped our second pregnancy would be the end of our infant loss journey, this journey continued when I began a complicated pregnancy with our second baby girl in March of 2016. Despite multiple ER visits and surgery to prevent premature labor, doctors were unable to prevent our second daughter, Madison Nicole Hogan, from joining her sister in Heaven after only five minutes of life in our arms. She was born on July 30, 2016, at twenty weeks and five days, just three weeks after her sister's first birthday.

Where was God in the midst of all of this? How could He have allowed this to happen to us when our hearts were so focused on helping to fulfill His will for both Niya and Madison?

Though my husband and I thought of ourselves as strong Christians, these tragedies forced us to grip every ounce of faith we had. Nothing shakes your foundation more than your worst fear happening twice, and within a year's time frame. We were devastated and had so many questions.

How can one process burying one child, let alone two in a one-year period? We knew God had led us to begin trying. Why would He lead us to try something He knew would not work out? I felt set up, deceived by the One I trusted most. I've always prided myself in having a close relationship with the Holy Spirit. Why didn't He warn me, or at least give me a heads-up that this would happen?

I thought I had prayed God's Word over our babies. Shouldn't this have yielded profitable results? At least, that is what I was taught in church as I learned how to build my faith. Yet, our prayers were not met with a baby. Although many of those questions remain unanswered, God used this time to draw me closer to Him by teaching me a lesson about faith that I want to share with you.

Sometimes we place pressure on ourselves to be in faith in order to see the manifestations of God. This achievement-faith mindset causes us to minimize God's power and sovereignty by focusing too closely on the results of what our faith can bring, rather than what the process of having faith takes us through. Sometimes the process is the point.

While I don't believe God caused the death of my daughters, I do believe nothing happens that He doesn't allow. Suffering happens simply because we live in a fallen world of sin that God never intended for us. But, because of Adam and Eve's sin, we live in this imperfect world until we meet Jesus in Heaven.

I had lost sight of this, which caused my initial reaction after our losses to be more focused on what my faith did not achieve than lamenting the hurt I truly felt. I felt ashamed that my prayers had failed. I wanted to push through so that I could be an example of God's goodness. I wanted the "I have overcome the world" part of John 16:33 without the "in this world you will have trouble" aspect. But God showed me that He is still present in our sufferings. And while He hates to see us hurt, He is close to us during those times and desires to use them to further enhance the intimate relationship He created us for. Going through the process of healing was something I had to do. Quoting scriptures to try and "be in faith" wasn't what He needed from me. He needed the pure, uninhibited Brittany to tell him how hurt she was so that He can be the Daddy God that He has always desired to be in these moments. It wasn't until I began to accept this renewed mindset that I was able to truly lament and begin the healing process.

I had to learn to bring the realities of all my hurt to God without putting scripture Band-Aids on each wound. I had to intentionally acknowledge my hurt to God first before a healing scripture could be used to continue to enhance my intimacy with Christ. While quoting scripture is imperative for increasing faith, true intimacy comes when we can simply curl up in Daddy God's arms and cry. Once He has healed your hearts, He will help to repair the foundation of your faith with scripture—but healing comes first.

Books like *Heart Made Whole* by Christa Black Gifford and *No More Faking Fine* by Esther Fleece taught me the vitality of lamenting before God. In Esther's book, she says, "If we minimize our suffering to a 3 on the pain scale, then we only heal at a 3 as well." Through this quote I realized that I had been trying to "push through" or "fake fine" so that I could be a good Christian again by showing God's faithfulness in my life rather than the current devastation.

Pushing through doesn't show God's faithfulness, it shows that we don't fully trust Him. In order for Christ to be your Lord, you must trust Him with even your deepest sorrows, knowing that it was never His desire that you experience such hurt. I'm so thankful that "we do not have a high priest who is unable to empathize with our weaknesses, but we have one who has been tempted in every way, just as we are . . ." (Hebrews 4:15, NIV). Jesus understands and wants our grief, and I am learning to bring it to Him fully. Through this understanding, God is truly healing our hearts and allowing us to live an honest life before Him. Healing is a process that only lamenting can carry us through, and I feel it is now a part of my purpose to share this truth.

So, where was God when I lost my daughters, and where was He during your loss? He was on the throne, ruling in His sovereignty, as always (Psalm 103:19). He was also right where He has always been, next to me with open arms, waiting to cry with me, because He was hurt at the thought of watching me endure such pain; Jesus is close to the brokenhearted and catches every tear in a bottle (Psalm 34:18 and 56:8).

Your healing can only be found when you bring the trueness of your heart to Jesus. I pray that, whatever you are walking through today, you are able to completely give your laments to Jesus. He wants to heal your heart. Please let Him in.

I'm not sure what devastations you have experienced in life that may allow you to identify with my pain, but my prayer is that, through this chapter, you are able to gain freedom from what your hurt has caused you to believe about where God is during these hurtful times. Regardless of your circumstances, I know from experience that He is close to the brokenhearted and only needs to be invited in to be the healer He has always desired to be for you.

LEARNING TO LOVE

by Michelle Wilson

My past has never been something I have been proud to talk about or have wanted to talk about. It doesn't often bring back joyful memories, but rather pictures of hurt, sadness, and sorrow. You see, my childhood was not a typical childhood. My parents separated when I was four years old, and this is when things got crazy for me. Always a daddy's girl, I felt lost in a fog when my parents were no longer together. I was dealing with not having my dad in my daily life, and it was traumatic; of course, I didn't know or understand that until many years later. After their divorce, my family went through a series of events that had me exposed to a world where fear was the norm. I saw and experienced many things that a child should not, including people trying to hurt the ones I loved, loved ones hurting each other, and other traumatic events. When the decision was made for us to relocate to the South after the divorce, it seemed that things would be better; but this hope was short lived, as I began to see the effects of alcoholism and mental illness on family members that were close to us. More fear, more anxiety.

At age eleven, in search of a better life, my mother moved us to another part of town with a man who would become her husband; even after a promise to me that it would never happen, she married him secretly. Anger and hurt were my new friends. Fear soon joined the anger and hurt as we faced emotional, mental, and physical abuse at the hands of my stepfather until I left home at eighteen. It was like a prison to me, so cold, frigid, always walking on eggshells, not knowing if something I said or did would trigger violence. Not knowing if the phone lines would be disconnected so that we could not call for help.

The life I imagined for myself was quite the opposite. I dreamed of getting married, having a very supportive family and children. A marriage and a family that loved each other and showed it, supported each other, and had no secrets.

Learning to love myself, overcoming the events of my childhood, proved to be one of the biggest challenges of my life. It manifested in every area of my life: spiritually, emotionally, and physically. The events from my childhood, teen years, and early adult life caused a state of being that overshadowed everything else. I defined my worth by my circumstances, by how others viewed me, and by my outward appearance. It was all a bleak picture to me. I didn't love me or even know how to love me. When I looked in the mirror

I did not see value. That reckless and skewed image I had of myself caused me to lead a life of impulsive decisions, searching for love in many of the wrong places. I was being promiscuous in hopes of being valued and loved, hoping that someone would think I was worth keeping. I was bouncing from relationship to relationship and, at times, juggling more than one relationship at a time. My life seemed like one bad decision after another. The challenge was learning to understand that I was destined and created for more and seeing myself as a confident, assured, worthy, beautiful woman.

I was in a place of internal despair and hopelessness. I learned to hide my inner turmoil by keeping up my "normal" life on the outside, while internally all I felt was shame. I believed every lie the people from my past told me about my character. All I could see was every inappropriate action. The hurt, pain, rejection, and fear consumed me. The obstacles and circumstances that I dealt with as a child, along with being involved in relationships that were unhealthy just to have something to cling to, led me to find myself in a dark place. I denied my own pain and hurt. I wrote it off as nothing. I would not allow myself to feel that pain, or even to deal with how I truly felt. I lied to myself and wore a mask to avoid dealing with my real issues.

In my early twenties, I found myself in church, saved, hoping this would be the fix for my painful past and the source to fill the hole in my heart. I quickly began the busyness that many new Christians experience of involving myself in many church activities and committees. For a while, this satisfied me. It felt like I had changed, but it was only on the surface. My heart matters were still very present. I still struggled with my past and with loving myself.

What made this time period even more difficult was that it seemed like these things were easy for other Christians. So why did I still struggle with these issues? Did no one else experience these struggles and conflicts? Why wasn't I instantly changed? How could I follow all the rules of being a Christian?

As I arrived at these questions, I drew from what I had learned in the past about God. As an early believer, I saw God as very distant and angry with me for the choices I made. I knew God was the Creator of the world, but I did not know or believe that He had a personal interest in me. Yes, I was saved, but I thought that was it. God was still a very big, intimidating dictator, one who expected me to make the right decision all the time—and if I didn't, He would not, could not, love me. I did not understand His love was unconditional.

During this period, I felt that life as I experienced it was as it was supposed to be. I wore a mask of laughter and insincere smiles. I hid from the world because that is what I had learned and what I thought pleased God, but on the inside I was miserable. I felt like I was dying, but I didn't know how to live.

One of the most vivid memories I have is walking into a store, where an older woman smiled at me and asked "how are you?" I was severely depressed, but didn't know it at the time and wouldn't have been able to articulate it to anyone. I put on a half-smile and after what seemed like an eternity, I finally responded, with tears in my eyes and a lump in my throat, "I am fine." But that wasn't what I wanted to say, it wasn't how I felt or the state I was in. I wasn't fine. I was broken and I felt I was at the end of my rope. I wanted to be honest in that moment and I couldn't. I was screaming on the inside, "I'm not fine! Help me, God!" So there I was, pretending to be okay again, the same thing I had always done. My mind told me that I was broken and could not be fixed, that even going to church would not help me.

While I wrestled with trying to understand what I was going through, I also tried to make sense of those around me. I was angry with and hurt by my dad for seemingly abandoning me, and my mother for marrying a man who victimized me. I struggled to try and make sense of all that had taken place, all that had led to me having a very skewed vision of myself and who I was. I felt unloved and misunderstood; there was no trust and I felt like an outsider, isolated and alone. I tried to convey to my parents how I felt, but my concerns fell on deaf ears. I came to a place where I was conflicted. I felt like I didn't know what God wanted or how I could please Him. What was the formula? What was I missing? I sometimes thought that this was how God wanted me to be. On the other hand, I also began questioning if there was more for me. Was it true that I would never experience true joy or have a family of my own? I even asked God how

I could learn to love myself. This is where things changed for me; I wanted to know what it was like to lead a life where I was enjoying being me. I did not want to live to please others or be concerned about what others thought. I wanted a life where I was healed from the pain of the past. Right or wrong, I began to challenge God.

When I started to open my heart to God, I didn't know what I was in for. I didn't even fully understand what I was embarking on—I just knew I needed something different. The shift came very unexpectedly for me. I attended a women's conference because a friend had a roommate back out and she needed someone to step in—and that someone was me. It was there that I had my first encounter with God, and it shook my life in a positive way.

Before this, I had never experienced the presence of God, feeling His love and His power all at the same time. It was at that conference that a woman shared with me intimate details concerning my life that only God knew. I knew in that moment that God was real and I felt His presence like never before. I finally felt I had the power to overcome the negative and self-defeating thoughts that had plagued me for so long. I was delivered from focusing on my negative attributes, which was the catalyst for my lack of self-love. The smile on my face was genuine. My heart began to heal from the events of my past. It was an awakening, an enlightenment. This was a transformation that occurred in my mind and in my life. I stepped into a place of possibilities. Not only that, I embraced God as my Heavenly Father, as my Dad. I would later come to understand how that awakening would shape and define my purpose and my destiny.

I knew that, in order to keep the power that I had found, I had to stay connected to God and I had to deal with myself. This meant work! It wasn't easy to look at the pieces of my past, deal with them, and put things back together. Dealing with those pieces would be more than just a one-time occurrence; it would be continuous work to gain the freedom and power that God had shown me was possible. I had to ask God to show me my good, my bad, and my ugly. It was a battle; I wasn't always willing to do and didn't always embrace the work that had to take place. As I learned to surrender my life to God's love, however, I began to come into the understanding of my purpose. I began to see a path for my life. While it did not all unfold at one time, the process had begun.

The Bible talks about a peace from God that surpasses all understanding. I didn't really know what that meant until I embarked on overcoming this obstacle in my life. When life happened, and it did along the way, I would seek God; and it was amazing to me how He would make His presence known. When I would go through things, I remember those around me saying, "Michelle, you need to be concerned about this," or "You need to do something to fix the issue," or "Why aren't you worried about what is happening? How are you going to make it?" I would reply, "I don't know how this is going to work out, but I do know that God is going to work it out, and because of that I have peace."

My grandmother was instrumental to my spiritual growth and extremely supportive all my life. She was a rock that I trusted, and this challenge was no exception. She continued to speak life into me, even when I didn't see it. She prayed for me, and with her life and friendship demonstrated God to me. As I released my past to God, He began to show me that the pain I experienced wasn't about my parents not loving me; they did the best they knew to do given their circumstances, but I had to forgive them and not stay in that place of hurt. They also needed healing and to see God's love through me. My spiritual leaders and Christian friends were very encouraging during this time as well. I also sought out a Christian counselor because I knew that I could not process my past on my own, but needed to do so outside of my immediate family.

Once I accepted God's love for me, I relied on His direction to deal with and learn from my past. I knew that, to live a purposeful life, I had to see myself as God sees me; I had to forgive myself. It allowed and is still allowing me to remember God's attributes and who I am to Him. I have tasted the joy of the Lord and I know that there is where I want to abide. It is a continuing process to keep that mindset. I learned perfection is not His portion for me, or for any of us. In fact, it is not possible. Jesus was perfect and without sin, and He paid the price for my sins all because of the love God had for me.

There was no other price that could be paid. He died so that I could know God's love through His mercy and grace.

Today, as I look back, I can see how much I've grown. I no longer doubt His love for me; in fact, it is the motivation for my walking into my destiny and purpose. I truly understand that God's love is not harsh, it is gentle. Even when I went through the trials of my childhood, even in the moments where I absolutely didn't love me, He was with me. I experienced adoration from God, something I did not know. He adores me, and He adores you. Just the way we are.

The power that I have gained because of overcoming this is not what one might typically expect. The power of God has allowed me to see what He placed in me. It is a power that changed my life because He was and is present with me and will allow me to be the vessel by which other lives are changed. It is the boldness to tell my story and it is the confidence to share my pain. I now know that part of my purpose is to help other women heal from their hurts and rest in our Father's arms.

PAIN PRODUCES POWER

by Angel Bartlett

I was born in Newport News, Virginia, and I am guessing I was born healthy and happy, but honestly, I do not recall much about my life as a baby or toddler, and I don't have a lot of fond memories of my childhood. From what I've been told and what I remember, I had a very difficult life from early on. My father had gone to prison for armed robbery and I would later learn that my mother was a drug addict. Although I never knew the exact reason, I do remember my sister and I going to live with our paternal grandparents at a very young age. I often tell people that I never had a chance to be a child. I have no memories of that time that make my heart smile—but I have plenty that remind me of how strong I am whenever my adult life tries to knock me down or steal my power, purpose, and peace.

I don't recall ever being with my mother when I was a baby. I do remember her coming to visit us and bringing nice clothes, shoes, and candy. Every time she left, I would run down the driveway, tears streaming down my face, begging, "Mommy, please don't go. Come back, I want to go with you!" At the end of a visit with my mom, my whole attitude would change. I would be very mean to my grandparents, because I thought they were the ones who kept us from living with our mother. I would see the hurt on my grandparents' faces, but no matter how negative my actions were, they would always console me. It was almost as though my grandmother wanted to tell me the entire story, but she could not bring herself to break my heart. She would just allow me to sob and comfort me when she could. I never understood why months would go by without seeing my mom, but no matter how long the days or the hours, I longed to have her in my life.

As the years went by, my grandparents of course grew older and my grandmother suffered several strokes. Eventually, they sat me and my sister down and told us we would have to go and live with our mother. I was sad my grandmother's health was declining, but elated to finally live with my mother.

Moving in with my mom, her boyfriend, and my little brother would prove to be a complete culture shock for both me and my sister. We moved from a single-family home to a trailer and quickly learned that something was not "right" about my mother. There was a major difference between visiting with her periodically and living with her full-time. My mother was a crackhead. While living with her I was subjected to physical abuse, mental abuse, sexual abuse, neglect, and her rage. My mother was not able to meet my or my sister's most basic needs, and I don't think she knew how. She was addicted to drugs and would do anything to get her next fix. She would leave us at home for days at a time without us knowing where she was or even if she was returning. I recall so many days of going without food or clean clothes. I hated going to school because the other children always made fun of my shoes. Sometimes my mother would return in a rage and want my sister and I to wait on her hand and foot. If I made one mistake or looked at her wrong, she would beat me with her fist, pull my hair, and call me terrible and profane names. At this stage in my life I heard those names more than I heard my birth name, Angel.

After multiple visits with social workers, my sister and I were eventually removed from my mother's care and introduced to a system called "child welfare." Life, however, did not get any better. I was shuffled through the system, moving between relatives, foster homes, group homes, and detention centers. I was angry and in and out of therapy. I believe the only thing that kept me sane was the seeds of God that had been planted in me by my grandparents when I was a little girl. I was running with drug dealers, getting shot at, constantly running from the police, and I had absolutely no sense of my own identity. Through all of this, in my darkest moments, when I took a second to cry, I knew something or someone was watching over me, because I would not die.

When I met my middle school principal, Carolyn Rose Tigell, my life started changing for the better; she was heaven-sent and truly a woman after God's own heart. She was not a foster parent, but her heart was very much attached to me. At the age of fourteen or fifteen, I was serving an eighteen-month bid up-state for an assault on several police officers. Ms. Tigell wrote a letter to the State of Virginia requesting that I be allowed to move with her to Florida. It was not long before those shackles were removed and I was on a plane to Florida. I had no idea that leaving Virginia would change my life forever. I was an angry, battered, broken child who did not care about much of anything or anyone; however, there was something about this woman that a small piece of me trusted and loved.

Moving to Florida did not heal my brokenness or the things stolen from me as a child. It is, however, the place where healing began and where I started learning more about the Word of God. I first began attending chapel services in the detention center and Mom Tigell would always send me inspirational scriptures and books. Even though I never really attended school, I was an avid reader and writer because it gave me so many different places of escape. In Florida I felt safe, protected, and loved. I felt like this total stranger loved me authentically; it was not about a paycheck. I recall waking up many nights from my frequent nightmares and finding Mom Tigell laying on the floor at the end of my bed, praying. Her presence and prayers would give me a "peace that surpasses all understanding," even though at the time I did not really know or fully understand what that meant. All I knew was that I felt at peace, and this would soon become my daily cry to God whenever the waters of life would begin to trouble me: "Please give me peace."

I would later go further on my path to healing and discover that my pain had purpose. I eventually earned my GED, got into community college, and from there earned a four-year college degree in sociology and later a master's in social work. I still had pain, but my purpose was much stronger than any pain I had ever experienced in my life. I understood this more as I continued to grow in my faith. I grew to love the book of Job because his life closely resembled mine in such a strong and powerful way. I wanted to have faith like Job; I wanted to be able to look back on my past, my pain, and be thankful, knowing that it would allow my future to be even greater.

As an adult, I grew deeper in my relationship with God; I longed to trust Him more and to build up my faith. I was often preached to about "the call" on my life, but before man ever spoke to me, God had already spoken to me. I accepted my call into ministry and began preaching the gospel, but I was in a war with two different people pulling at my heart, God and the "devils" of my past. As much as I loved God, I continued to struggle with lust and relationships. Despite all of my healing and discovery, I found myself in wrong relationships, struggling to make connections or find meaningful relationships. Somehow, I attracted broken men who in return would try to further break me. I was on fire for God and knew that no one saved me, healed me, or delivered me but God, but I did not trust Him enough to send me my Boaz as God did for Ruth. This often kept me repenting.

I learned quickly that sometimes hurt caused by the church is the worst hurt one can ever experience, especially when your background is one such as mine. One would expect people in the church, in ministry, including preachers, to be different, but the truth is they are people, too, and all have their own stories, trials, and tribulations. Unfortunately, the church added further hurt and condemnation to my already fractured life, so I backslid out of the church. I was sick of the "holier than thou" and judgmental people and, most importantly, I did not like feeling as though I was trapped in a box and unable to speak my truth. No matter where you are or what your title is, if you cannot speak your truth then you cannot ever experience true freedom.

In my backsliding, I introduced myself to additional layers of pain. I felt like if I was going to sin, I might as well sin really well, so I did just that. In doing so, I found yet another lesson that I must learn, one that I am currently still learning. For years I have been a counselor to many, but I never really took the time to seek out additional counseling for myself to explore the "why" behind my actions. I believe that many times we stay trapped in a box because we are afraid to be found out, afraid of either others or ourselves finding the truth. We are afraid of what other people will think if they really knew the truth. But the real truth is what the Bible teaches us, that the truth will set us free.

I can tell you from my own personal experience that the truth will sometimes, in most cases, hurt deeply, but if you allow yourself to discover the real you and set your mind, heart, spirit, and soul to be dedicated to the process, you will come out a winner. A winner sometimes falls, but they always have the ability and tenacity to get back up again. What I have learned about myself in my quiet time with the Most High God is that, if it did not kill me back when I was a child—helpless, hopeless, and without those who were supposed to be looking after me and caring for me—it certainly cannot kill me now. I am responsible for my own outcome and I am determined that the outcome will lead me where God has predestined me to be, long before I was formed in the belly of the womb (Jeremiah 1:5). I am a woman that is fearfully and wonderfully made.

In closing, I want to remind every reader, every sister and every brother, that life's circumstances do not determine your outcome. You have the power and ability to speak to any mountain and tell that mountain to move. If you say it with faith and you really believe in your heart that the mountain cannot stay, I can testify that it shall be moved (Mark 11:23). I am on a never-ending journey to fulfill my destiny of power, purpose, and peace. I know what my purpose is, and I know the source of my power, and I know what it feels like to truly walk in peace that surpasses all understanding; not just some, but all understanding. I have a plan to experience that for the rest of my life, and I want to encourage you to do whatever it takes to develop a similar plan and stick to it. You can lose the weight, you can be healthy, you can be happy, you are worthy, you are forgiven, you are strategic, you are talented, you are desired, you are not sad, you are not depressed, you are worthy of the call! You are worthy of living a peaceful and prosperous life, because you are a survivor—and together, we got this!

LIFE OF CONFUSION, BUT SAVED BY FAITH

by Tammy Rowe

I am a registered nurse, born and raised in Virginia. Growing up, my childhood had its ups and downs. Being the youngest of four made life lonely at times because of the twelve-plus year age difference between myself and my siblings. Coming from a family who struggled with addiction, my outlook was different from a typical child my age. I spent a great deal of time alone, so I had to mature quickly and deal with things that a child my age shouldn't have had to go through. I began to become aware of addiction around fifth grade. I noticed behavior and appearance changes in my family and had to deal with it head-on because my siblings were older and out of the house. Growing up, we moved around frequently, so strong friendships with children my age were few and far between. Not having anyone to talk to that could relate to me and my feelings, I began writing in my diary to release my pain. Fast forward to my high school years; I really began to understand how the addiction was affecting the people around me. Although I was a cheerleader, flag girl in the marching band, and did things that other teenagers did, I still felt alone and broken inside due to a lack of connection with my family. The one thing I did not understand was why I never felt a strong, loving connection with the people I thought would love me the most, my family.

After moving around, having to live in a hotel temporarily, my family finally became stable again and was able to move into a neighborhood where I made quite a few friends. I made a friend who I could relate to because addiction haunted his family as well. We became good friends, but the circumstances of life took us in different directions as we went into adulthood. We lost contact for many years, not knowing that we would reunite years later.

I had big dreams! I knew that I wanted to go to college and travel the world, to do all the things I was promised as a child but never got a chance to do. I dreamed of being a wealthy lady, with a big house on several acres of land, bright green grass, and a pool in the backyard. Getting married was also on the list, but I did not want children. I didn't want children because I was afraid of what the world was becoming, and I did not want to bring a child into the world to suffer like I felt I did.

I eventually enrolled in college but never completed anything. I jumped from college to college, job to job, searching for success without a solid plan of how to reach my final destination. I never understood that I had to get focused to figure out who I really was and where I was going. I also found myself looking for love in all the wrong places, ending up in unhealthy and abusive relationships that took a toll on me. I was trying to fill the voids that had consumed me since childhood, and the road to figuring out what I really wanted and needed wasn't easy.

By the time I turned twenty-six, I was married to my first husband, a mother to two young children, and serving as a licensed practical nurse. While my ultimate goal was to become a registered nurse, I wouldn't achieve that until almost a year or so later. You would think my life was what I wanted it to be, but deep down inside, my life was dark and extremely lonely. There was a lack of emotional connection between my husband and I that existed before we even actually got married; however, I felt obligated to go through with it because my family had already invested money in the wedding. I didn't want to disappoint our family and friends who were anticipating the big wedding day, so I ignored my doubts and fears about moving forward.

Before and during the marriage, my husband had cheated on me with multiple women and was also emotionally and physically abusive. I often felt like he didn't care about me and that I was merely a benefit. He would be gone all the time, would turn off his phone and act suspicious. My role in the marriage was to obey him; when things didn't go his way or when I responded to his antics in a way he disagreed with, he'd assault me. There were times I'd be pushed or hit with an extension cord, and once he even attempted to smother me with a pillow. I don't want to paint the picture that I didn't fight back, I did, but I grew tired and weary from the fighting. So, eventually, I filed for divorce.

Up to that point, I had faced many challenges and always dealt with them by removing myself from people who I felt had nothing positive to contribute to my life. I was divorced and free from what I thought was the most miserable point in my life. A few months after my divorce, I reunited with my childhood friend. After four years, we got married—but that marriage proved to be even more detrimental than my first, because he was suffering from addiction. I was aware of his addiction before the marriage, but I was trusting God and praying that things would get better. He also assured me that he had things under control and he was going to get help; however, throughout the marriage, I dealt with lies and feelings of guilt and disgust because of his addiction.

In 2015, we made a decision to move to Georgia in order to begin a new life together, help him with his addiction, remove us from negative influences, and get a breath of fresh air. I prayed, had hope as well as a ton of faith, but his addiction never stopped. My husband drove trucks for a living and I went three months without seeing him after our move to

Georgia. He would tell me he was in one state when he was really in another. More often than not, he'd lie to me about the amount of money he had and he rarely helped to support our family. To make matters worse, when my husband finally took a break off the road and came home to visit, I noticed his addiction had worsened while he was away. Seeing him was bittersweet, but while he was gone I had time to think about my own life. I told him that it was either rehab or the end of our marriage. Initially he agreed to rehab to keep me quiet, but it only ended up in us separating because he did not keep his promise.

Living in Georgia was one of my biggest challenges. I was dealing with my marital problems, with feelings and emotions, and with being all alone with nowhere to run. My life felt empty. There I was, in a big city with thousands of people, but no one to call family or friend. I had no other choice at that moment but to find myself. I felt I was doing all I could to keep my marriage and my life together, but nothing took away the pain I was feeling and nothing I tried to do made things better.

While dealing with all of that, I felt like a failure; I felt I had no purpose in life and I could not understand why I was going through all that madness. I began to question God, because I prayed and treated people like I want to be treated, but I still felt like I was suffering. I had no understanding as to why I was going through all of this. After attending church a few times, I felt ashamed because I had a fear of being judged and of the unknown. The pastor, along with other members of the church, however, made me feel welcome. I began to go to church more and pray more, and I gained an even better understanding of the things that had happened in my life. Well, at least I thought I had an understanding, but boy was I wrong.

Going to church and praying, but also being separated from my husband and feeling powerless and all alone with no family in a foreign place, caused me to believe I would lose my mind. I listened to sermon after sermon, but still felt confused because of my thoughts on divorce, that if I did so I would somehow disappoint God. What was I supposed to do? There I was, a grown, successful woman on the outside, but crying like a little girl on the inside. I had no one to talk to about my problems and I felt like I would burst if my life did not change.

Finally, I decided to open up and talk to people about my situation, only to hear them say to work on my marriage and that my marriage could withstand anything but abuse. With that advice, I stayed in my marriage. After deciding to do so, my husband and I reunited and decided to make things work. I continued going to church and we were approved to have our first home built. We did our best to make things better and I felt my life was headed down the right path. Things were good for a few weeks—only for me to notice the lies, the complaints of having no money, and the addiction taking over again. He refused all offers of going to church with me and made excuses as to why he did not want to go. He began to verbally abuse me and then began taking his frustration out on my son, his stepson, leading to a physical altercation between the two of them that left me with a broken toe.

At that point, I felt like I was back at square one, asking God "Why?" I was back to feeling like a loser, feeling powerless, and having no sense of peace; I was not sure what to do anymore. Confusion, anger, guilt, and disappointment buried me in a dark hole of regret. Even though I was questioning God about why it was happening, I learned by attending church that I had to lean on God more and cast all of my burdens upon Him. That statement is easier said than done, but I had no other choice but to remain focused, keep my cool, and let God take control.

I finally realized and understood that God was the only true friend I had to run to for help, and He had been with me all along. Still going to church and maintaining my spiritual beliefs, listening to sermon after sermon, I knew my life had to change, and that I was the person responsible for initiating the change in my life. After moving into my brand new home, my husband's verbal abuse and mood swings continued. I later found out that his anger was being taken out on both of my children when I was at work. On one occasion, I had to have him arrested. He had become angry and was cursing at my ten-year-old daughter. When I inquired about his rude and disrespectful behavior, he spat in my face. My fourteen-year-old son ran downstairs to my rescue and he then attacked my son, leaving my son's face swollen and my arm bruised from standing over my son while blocking the blows that were being thrown by my husband.

Once his aggression decreased, my husband ran upstairs. In an attempt to keep my kids safe, I told my son to go outside and walk toward the end of the driveway as I went upstairs to get my daughter. My husband then ran downstairs, jumped in my car, stomped on the gas, and attempted to run my son over with my car. My son jumped out of the way as my husband sped off recklessly. I called 911 and they responded immediately. While waiting for the police to arrive, my husband came back and told me to take my car and give him the keys to his vehicle. I gave him his keys to keep the peace. He then jumped back in my car and yelled an expletive while sticking up his middle finger, then sped off. The police arrived shortly after he left—they were able to find him, retrieve my car, and arrest him.

After all of the torture I had been through, I finally heard God speak. God said, "Let him go." Immediately, all my feelings of confusion, anger, guilt, and disappointment were washed away. As he was put in handcuffs and taken away, I felt like a load had been lifted and I could finally exhale, so I filed for divorce.

The moral of this story is, you must understand that the mindset of an individual who suffers from addiction can drain you mentally and spiritually. Sometimes we are addicted to what we think is love and chaos because we have never experienced true love and peace. You have to understand when to let go and let God take control. My biggest problem through everything was not knowing when God was talking to me. I asked God so many times for guidance, but I did not know when it was God speaking. As I look back, God was trying to show me my ex-husband's true colors all along, but I was confused with what the church said about divorce, about saving my marriage and letting go. I really should not have married him in the first place, because God wasn't the foundation of the marriage and I did not seek guidance from God until after we married; therefore, I wasn't able to discern whether or not he was the man for me. If you involve God in everything from the beginning, you will know when something is for you. God is a God of love and peace, not worry, confusion, and frustration.

I encourage you to never regret the hard times that come your way. I believe God is using my story to help you. I am here to empower you! Remember, through your pain and struggles God is conditioning you for the blessing that is about to come over your life. Keep in mind, God will remove people out of your life and shift things around that may cause emotional and physical hurt, because when God blesses you, not everyone is meant to celebrate those blessings with you. God has better for you, so know your worth and put God first in every move you make from the moment you end this chapter. Be patient and watch where God will take you! Be blessed!

THE MARRIAGE PERFORMANCE

by Dana Reed

One summer when I was eleven years old, I found myself in a youth orchestra camp as a violinist. The camp wasn't for beginners, and, wouldn't you know it, there was a performance at the end of the camp. Can you imagine being in a class where there's no teacher, no instructor, feeling lost, attempting to play an instrument, playing the wrong notes in the wrong key, having no help? That was me. I couldn't play a single note. I was clueless the entire time.

On "performance" day, I was on stage, ready to perform. I don't know how many musical selections we played—or should I say, they played—but there I was, the imposter, misfit, or whatever, "playing" too. All along I played the wrong notes in the wrong key. No one asked me how I got that far uninterrupted . . . . No one even noticed. I showed up, I was in place, I looked the part, but I was LOST!

Playing the wrong notes in the wrong key in summer camp is pretty harmless, but it actually became the script for the way I patterned my life. Now, consider your mental programming over the years, what shapes your thoughts and beliefs, as that sheet of music played in the orchestra performance called "Life." How would you feel if you'd been playing the wrong notes all along? Pretty heartbroken, right? Well, that was me. It was not only harmful, it also had costly consequences.

At the age of twenty-three, I married. My new sheet of music was "and the two shall become one" (Mark 10:8). I repeated this scripture many times. I thought I knew what it meant, but I was clueless. I frequently asked my husband the question, "What are we going to do to become one?" As the years ticked by, I didn't see any fruit of that union. I'm not speaking of children per se, I couldn't bear children, I'm referring to the product of the union of two becoming one. There was nothing of substance between us, just passing years. We were merely coexisting.

I recall one day standing at the kitchen sink, thinking, "I don't want to be fifty years old in a marriage like this, just empty." We weren't becoming one, but we certainly were becoming something. I had my thoughts about marriage, he had his, and neither were God's thoughts. It was the complacency and my feelings of being taken for granted that opened the door for rejection to come in. So, I took a passive role in restoring the marriage.

In a marriage where a husband and wife actively participate in their roles, there would have been dialogue and communication to resolve issues. We never took that approach. Our marital roles were lacking in growth, love, respect, communication, and compromise. I took an active role in preserving myself, a single mindset, as the two of us never became one. You see, I grew up in a family that wasn't "touchy feely" in showing love, but a strong sense of family and belonging was instilled. My environment said, "I belong!" Then there was the church. I'm a church baby, so as I grew and matured, I embraced my family values and church teachings. The strong ties to the acceptance I felt within my family and church made it impossible for me to accept the rejection I experienced in my marriage. I knew that the way that I was being treated did not align with my beliefs. There was a core value system that wasn't being upheld in my marriage and I couldn't get used to that.

Beyond that, we were both complacent about correcting the marital issues. To compound this, we had no knowledge of how to apply biblical principles to the marriage. Furthermore, I would later discover, there was a strong effect on me from having had an absent father. There was a void that lurked in my subconscious, and I had lived without the example of a good marriage. I came into the marriage looking for headship, for leadership, without having had a clear distinction demonstrated in my own life by my father. I did not know how leadership should look, either between a father and a daughter or between a husband and a wife, which produced a void my ex-husband could never fill. The marriage lasted about six years. Yes, we were Christians and marriage is supposed to be "until death do you part," but we decided to go our separate ways.

For the next seven years I was single again. My initial years as a newly single woman were filled with religion. I would pick and choose biblical truths for life application until the Lord led me to rededicate my life. I started growing in my relationship with God.

I remarried seven years later, in my late thirties, assuming that I was a different person that time. I said to myself, "I've got this now." Can you imagine my excitement about having another chance to marry, this time God's way? I thought I had dotted my i's and crossed my t's. I was drawn to the idea of being a couple that served God, living "Thy kingdom come here on earth" in church ministries and in business. Things were fine, on the surface, for many years. I had learned from my past, or so I thought.

Apparently, I wasn't the only one with issues. In hindsight, I am baffled by our thoughtless attention to following God's plan for marriage. My husband and I operated as though we had no power to impact the course of our train wreck when we were the conductors! Soon we began functioning as roommates, empty of love on the inside, stuck on past thoughts, unresolved issues, and preconceived notions. I was met with the thorn in my side again, rejection! We were two broken people not able to grab each other by the hand and go to God, who could have repaired the breach.

Genesis 2:24 says, "Therefore shall a man leave his father and his mother, and shall cleave unto his wife: and they shall be one flesh." In all my getting married, I had missed the first half of Genesis 2:24. There was no "leaving and cleaving" in my marriage. I continued to have my morning devotions without a targeted focus. I prayed amiss, wrongly. I did not seek God for answers to my crumbling marriage, acting as if I wasn't at all responsible for its condition. I didn't know that, in Christ, I could be fine in many areas of my life, yet on life support in others. I prayed alone at revivals and conferences for my marriage to be restored.

Recall how I thought during my first marriage that I didn't want to be fifty years old in an empty marriage? Well, strangely enough, I was fifty-two years old, living in a failing marriage for the second time. If you don't learn from your mistakes, history will repeat itself. Sad but true. I didn't peel back the layers to identify what was in my soul. My second marriage didn't survive. There I was again, separated then divorced after fourteen years of marriage. You may ask what was wrong. I continued playing the wrong notes, in the wrong key, hoping and praying for an outcome I had rehearsed and practiced without proper instruction. The problem was, marriage required something more of me than I realized I needed to give—and being an imposter wasn't going to suffice. While I thought I was doing the right things, I still didn't have it quite right.

I prayed and rehearsed "and the two shall become one" over and over. I thought I knew what that part of the verse, Genesis 2:24, meant, but I was clueless. The unifying of a couple doesn't just happen. I had put God in a box. That scripture became my prayer and consumed my thoughts; I verbalized it until I performed the words (erroneously) in my marriage. It was just like the violin. I played that scripture on center stage, with the wrong notes in the wrong key, like the eleven-year-old me, all over again.

I took my marriage to prayer, but I should have taken myself to prayer and asked, "God, what am I doing wrong?" Sure, my spouse and marriage needed prayer, but first and foremost God needed to work on me. The thought that I wasn't the problem was, in fact, the problem. I found myself at revivals and conferences praying for my marriage to be restored. I should have prayed with my husband, not in isolation, even if he wasn't participating.

It took me two divorces and a third relationship that was *headed* for marriage, which likely would have ended in divorce, before I saw my mess. My power to see was emerging. In the third relationship, all of the red flags were there, signs that the marriage wouldn't go well. I ignored the signs many times as the relationship experienced the "on and off again" rituals. I continued to ask God to show me if my potential third husband was meant for me. I kept asking Him even though I failed to heed His answers. While I didn't give up or give in to Satan, I was at war with my flesh. The tendency to struggle, to wrestle ourselves to the ground, is something we must all deal with, but there was power in my praying. The Spirit answered each time until I finally heeded the promptings of God. It was in the rituals of this latest relationship that I recognized my core value system for the first time. That third marriage didn't occur because of the power of the Lord and His Spirit within me, which turned my propensity for an "I do" into a "not again."

I never gave thought to the entire verse of Genesis 2:24, nor dissected it on a deeper than surface level, even though I clung to it for a number of years as my blueprint for marriage. God showed me that my focus was isolated. A deeper look into this entire verse and other scriptures throughout the Bible revealed a plan and path for couples to navigate on the journey to becoming one. It was more than just an act or a score to play.

I struggled to see the peace in my situation—and why I had to go this route, I do not know. Frankly, my pastor had to help me to understand, because I was attached to the misery of being twice divorced. But my eyes were finally opened to the truths in my failed marriages. Yes, I failed in my marriages, but I'm not a failure. My peace is that I learned where I wasn't fully present physically, emotionally, and spiritually in my marriages, and because of that revelation there would be no more mindless marriages.

I'm awake now. I praise God that the third marriage didn't happen and that He allowed me to see the trap set for me. God shined His light beneath the surface of my truth to expose Satan's lies and God's truth. I was able to rise from under Satan's trap and my own deception. I can truly see God now.

I'm now in a better place, having been clearly told my purpose by God through all of my missteps. When we know our purpose and operate accordingly, Satan fails at his attempts to steal from us. Our challenge is to go beneath the surface and deal with the dark places until Christ is formed in us; to allow people in our space to sharpen us, "as iron sharpens iron," to grow us. My purpose is to share my experience so that couples may reflect on their "performance." Our purpose is God-given. Individually we are of value and precious in God's sight. As married couples, though, you are also a symbol. Marriage is a great glimpse of salvation, two becoming one, Jesus coming into our lives and our lives becoming one in marriage.

I can speak on both sides of the marital fence because I'm single *again,* but not a bitter woman damaged by marriage and hating life. I'm one who still loves God's institution of marriage and would joyfully welcome God's blessing of a mate and marriage done God's way. Whether single or married, the celebration is that I'm conscious and hearing what the Spirit speaks in my heart. I will encourage couples as an insider from the outside. I've lived both worlds *twice*, and God has a message in me to give to you. Ask God questions in multiple ways and listen to your heavenly Father in order to play the right notes in the right key, tuned in to the Conductor of your soul for your marriage—"not my will but Thy will be done."

My mess is my message to you and the *purpose* for which I write this chapter. Christians and Christian marriages don't succeed by accident; you have to be intentional. Satan comes to steal, kill, and destroy anything God creates, and marriage is top on Satan's list. Do you see signs in your life or marriage that things may be heading off key? Reorder some things if necessary. Better yet, grab your spouse by the hand and pray together! Christian marriage is not a stage performance, as some may think. Given the state of marriages in our day and time, some think it is a show that you can end and then recast. But in Christ's design, marriage is forever and is intended to model our relationship with Him, which is eternal. The couple is to love and cherish one another and each is to lay down their life for the other until death do them part.

I leave you with this—a gift God gave to me that I neglected during my marriages:

AMISS

I played AMISS—my instrument—
wrong notes, wrong key

This sheet of music was in my head, it's
what I read, it sounded right to me

Could it be, this was meant for me,
planned—for my Destiny?

Nooo, the Creator planned my score, but
the enemy sat on the floor—

He crafted his notes, ever so close, that
my ears played his the most

A subtle deception is all that was needed
for the YEARS

I Played AMISS

Until the Conductor had me see
the trap set for me

For years I conducted the enemy's
score—wrong notes, wrong key

Two divorces through this score . . .
Mmm and headed for one more

Before I saw, through His grace, that enemy
sitting right there on the floor

This sheet of music in my head, the
score I *played* . . . AMISS . . .

Was a scripture I prayed amiss found in Genesis 2:24.

Now you have the blueprint to understand the consequence of being an imposter, but you also have the tools to heed instruction and play the right notes in the right key. The audience is watching. My clarion call is that we have an audience of one, God. Marriage is His score, so read from His sheet of music.

AGAINST ALL ODDS, LOVE PREVAILED

by Evangela "Van" Ruffin-Williams

I moved into my first home excited and in shock that the brick home sitting at the end of the cul-de-sac was all mine; I couldn't believe it was my time to finally own something. However, even as I was filled with both reminiscences of my past and hopes for my future while signing the closing papers, the truth was that I was broken and battered. Night after night I would look out of the window in the living room and wait for the lights from my husband's car to shine bright through the blinds, but too often it was another night where my husband didn't return from work. Worried and in fear of being embarrassed, I never voiced my concerns because I didn't want to hear "I told you so" from everyone, so I watched my house of love slowly turn into a house of turmoil and pain.

In the summer of 2003, I met an amazing man. We met through a friend, first talking online and then later exchanging numbers. He kept me laughing for hours and we began to talk about life, visiting each other quite frequently. After a few months, we decided to live together and get married. The Friday before we got married, though, he dropped me off at work and I didn't see him again until Saturday night—the night before our wedding. Yet I still wanted to go through with it, because I was worried about what others would say and think about me if I called it off. See, my soon-to-be husband was suffering from substance abuse, and everyone knew it, but I believed I could change him through marriage. Sadly, I was wrong—and I would also come to realize that I really needed to work on changing myself.

On Sunday, December 21, 2003, we got married. Even though there were signs our marriage would be shaky from the beginning, we both knew that there was something special that brought us together. Family and friends were skeptical, but in that moment none of them mattered. We wanted to make things work between us and we both held on to the hopes that we had finally found true love.

From 2004–2005, there were major fights between my husband and I. Almost every Thursday night, the night before payday, we would argue. These arguments would escalate to the point of us having a physical altercation or him leaving for two or three days to go on drug binges. He'd only return after he'd spent all of his paycheck or I'd go searching for him at his normal hangouts. On one of those occasions, when he returned from his binge, I was extremely upset that he had been gone for days with my vehicle, leaving me stranded at home. As we started arguing, I got into my vehicle, he jumped in with me, and I began to drive. When I eventually stopped the vehicle, he got out and came around to the driver's side, where our verbal fight became a physical altercation. We ended up in the middle of the street where he beat me badly—I had bruises on my back, neck, and face. This led to his arrest, a restraining order, and ultimately him serving six months in jail.

While one would think that incident would lead to our permanent separation, we would be reunited when he was released in the summer of 2005. I was reluctant and ashamed to share with anyone that I wanted my marriage to work, knowing they would disapprove, so I kept my decision mostly to myself, not even sharing it with my closest friends.

In January 2006, I decided we needed a fresh start, so we decided to move to another state to rebuild our marriage and give us the opportunity to depend on each other. There was a position opening in my company's Charlotte office, so I applied. We were excited for a fresh start—but, unfortunately, as we prepared for the move, old habits seemed to creep back into our lives. This time our constant fighting and making up revolved heavily around alcohol, mainly for me. I suppressed all of my feelings of anxiety, hurt, disappointment, and anger by using anything that had the words 80 proof finely printed on the label. Meanwhile, my husband was also still struggling with his addiction.

On Tuesday, February 21, 2006, my husband dropped me off at work and the kids at the babysitter, but we were never picked up. By that point I had had enough; I didn't really panic, just used it as a confirmation that I needed to leave with my children and start a new chapter. I was settled on moving on without my husband. The very next day I came home to find my home under contract after listing it the week prior. I said to myself, "It's on now! There is no turning back!"

I had concluded because of his disappearing act that my husband wasn't going to join us on our journey to Charlotte. Well, my husband finally showed up the night before we were scheduled to move. On the day of our move, my father suggested my husband come along to help us load and unload the truck. After arriving in Charlotte, we moved into a brand new townhome, which was far more expensive than I was prepared for. I said, "Lord, how am I going to do this by myself?" Then fear and doubt started to come into my spirit and I became nervous of the unknown. My father didn't feel comfortable leaving us by ourselves so he suggested that my husband stay. Well, during this time I was saying to myself, "He is down here now, so maybe it was meant to be?" This was my typical response even when things weren't truly going well; I'd be hopeful that everything would end up going great. I believed this was a fresh start and that we were going to be fine.

Everything wasn't fine, however; there was still something missing: *church*. We had visited a few but nothing felt right. I didn't want to be in a church where we would be just a number on a member list, but rather somewhere small, similar to my home church. A coworker suggested a small church with less than one hundred members. I reached out to them to talk more about their ministry, and on Sunday, August 13, 2006, we began fellowshipping at the church. We were faithful members to the church and participated in various departments within the ministry. Now we had the last element to make our transition complete and begin a journey toward a healthy family dynamic.

Things were going well; my husband even expressed a desire to own his own business, a goal I wanted to help him achieve. In February 2007, God blessed us to move into our dream home, which we referred to as the *big house*. Due to obstacles and challenges that I thought had been left in Virginia, though, the cycle began again. I can't blame all that went wrong in our marriage, particularly during that time, solely on my husband. In his time of weakness, I neglected and rejected him. Instead of trying to help him deal with what seemed like his toughest battle, I provoked him. Maybe because I didn't want to face my own demons, let alone his. It was tough to see him go through his battle, but I was blinded by my own misuse of alcohol, and our addictions slowly became our norm. At that point we had tried counseling and praying, but nothing was changing—yet I still pressed on as if everything was normal.

In August of 2007, we lost the *big house,* and I found my-self uprooting my three angels yet again to somewhere af-fordable. We remained active in the church, but meanwhile the issues my husband and I were battling became over-whelming. No matter what was said in the church service or how high the spirit was, we were lost. Every week I would pray and ask God to "take the taste away," but I never pre-pared my mind and heart for a transformation. I spent years battling between holiness and alcohol—I was living a dou-ble life. I felt like there was a spotlight that shined bright on my sins, so I often gave the loudest "amen" or "hallelujah" to wipe away any doubt about my sanctity. I would hear the pastor say, "Choose ye this day whom you shall serve" and I despised his words, because it was a constant reminder that I didn't have it all together. I led a life which seemed as if it was hopeful, but I was dying inside.

After months of attempting to put the pieces to our love puzzle together, we still weren't making progress. Financial setbacks, trust issues, and arguments were wreaking havoc in our home. I began to pray nonstop for God to change the course of our lives and save our marriage. My husband began to change, but in my mind it wasn't fast enough. I wanted him to do a complete 180, but meanwhile I was still facing my own addiction. During those months we tried to make our marriage work, but once again, we failed and again sep-arated in February 2010. Through the process, though, I did learn to pray, have faith, and seek Godly counsel.

In April 2011, due to stresses in my life, I had a mild stroke, which left my speech impaired and me out of work for several weeks. During that time, I was wondering if I should move back to Virginia where all of my family lived so I didn't place any further burden on my children. My husband contacted me because he heard that I was sick and wanted to know if he could come and take care of me. After speaking with him, I contacted my pastor and co-pastor for Godly counsel. My pastor thought it would be a great idea; my co-pastor had a few questions, but she wanted what was in my best interest.

My husband came back the summer of 2011 to help take care of me and was able to get his old job back. I believed things were finally going to work out for us. While I would faithfully pray for God to change my husband, I never asked God to change me. Because my husband had his issues, it was very easy for me to hide mine. His issues affected the family mentally, physically, and financially, and because he was the head of the family I put my focus more on him. Just as we thought things were back on track, however, he was back to his old habits. I finally said, "Enough is enough, I am done. I can't do this anymore." I was tired, broken, and stressed. In February 2013, we officially divorced and that chapter of my life was over—but God had another plan for me and my then ex-husband.

In May 2014, while at work, I received a call from my ex-husband because he had a dream about me and wanted to make sure I was okay. During that time, he and I were both in new relationships. He had been delivered from his past addictions and, even though I was currently in a relationship with my children's father and he was with someone from his past, the phone calls and frequent visits began. As things began to pick up and rebuild with my ex-husband I received the most devastating news. I had a phone call from my daughter letting me know that my mother had passed away. I called my ex-husband to let him know what happened. Almost every day we talked on the phone, and I can truly say he was there for me during one of the worst storms in my life. After my mother's memorial, my husband and I decided to put God first and make our marriage work. We went through counseling and he moved in on December 26, 2015, and we remarried on Tuesday, December 29. We are not perfect, but we are striving toward perfection. This has been a journey for the both of us and God continues to show us ourselves every day. Now I know how to communicate by talking to and with my husband, not at him. I'm learning that it's not my way or the highway; it is God's way or no way. Through this process we have learned that, through prayer and faith, nothing is impossible with God; we are living witnesses that, no matter what, love prevails.

BENT, NOT BROKEN
by Pamela Brunson

My journey began in January, 1990. I was hanging with my friend, Tiffany, when we decided to go out to the club—and that's where I met Mark. We were both in the military, and he was tall, handsome, and well dressed, just like I liked. We exchanged numbers, and that's when the whirlwind romance began. Mark swept me off my feet. We talked every chance we got and he told me everything I wanted to hear. The daily conversations eventually led to us visiting each other, and the time we spent together was magical. The more I was with him, the more I needed him. There was something about this man that was different than the others. He became my drug of choice. He was everything I prayed for and I looked forward to our daily conversations.

Before I met Mark, I spent most of my weekends in the clubs thinking I was having fun, searching for something I would never find. In reality, I just wanted to be loved unconditionally. I was tired of being by myself. The things I searched for, I thought I found in Mark. Our relationship moved very fast and everything fell into place. He wanted me to talk to his mother, which was a big deal to me. He and I continued to date and everything was good. Mark eventually received military orders to move out of the country, and that's when he asked me to marry him. He said he couldn't live his life without me and I felt the same.

Being young, I didn't realize there were so many red flags, starting with the proposal. I'm embarrassed to admit that when he asked me to marry him, the ring he proposed with wasn't new; I felt weird about it, but I ignored the feeling. I thought that as long as it was from him and he wanted me to be his wife, then all was well. He didn't want to have a big wedding so we decided to go to the courthouse.

When the wedding day arrived I felt dreadful; it was like my spirit knew this was a bad decision, and the feeling wouldn't go away. As we stood in front of the judge, everything in me said, "Don't do it! Leave!" I felt I had come too far not to go through with it, though. After all, he loved me, and he had asked me to marry him, right?

A few months after the wedding, Mark and I took a vacation to his hometown where I met the rest of his immediate family. That vacation would be the first time I experienced the darker side of him. The evening we arrived we went out to a club, and Mark was mingling and socializing with the people he knew from his hometown. I found myself sitting at the bar talking with his brother, thinking it would be acceptable. Mark later came up to me and said, "Let's go!" in a direct tone. I could tell he was angry but I didn't understand why. As we approached the door, he threw his beer in my face and pulled me outside to the car where our first fight happened. I had never been so embarrassed in my life; I was confused because, to my knowledge, I hadn't done anything wrong.

When we got back to his mother's house, I told her what happened then, I began packing my things to leave. His family begged and pleaded with me to give him another chance. My common sense was telling me to leave him, but my heart said stay and so I did. He said he was sorry and promised it would never happen again. I believed him. Once again, my spirit was speaking to me, but I was so caught up in his world that I ignored it. Little did I know that would be the beginning of a downward spiral.

A few weeks passed and the incident was still fresh in my mind. I considered getting a divorce but I found out I was pregnant with our first son. At that point, I felt obligated to stay, as I already had a young child, and now one was on the way. Things were a little rocky, but I thought if I just loved him enough things would be fine.

Eventually, Mark and I were stationed at the same place and I was excited, because I thought the distance had prompted our issues. My assumption was wrong. Being together brought on daily mental and physical abuse. I felt so isolated and alone, but I was determined to make him see that my love for him was real. As time went on, though, I could see the mental and physical abuse was bringing out the worst in me. I was in a very unhappy situation. I desperately wanted my husband to spend time with me, but all he was interested in was hanging out in the streets. As time went on the abuse continued to get worse. Not only was I dealing with the daily physical abuse, but I was also dealing with him cheating. With those two things coupled together I felt completely worthless. What kind of woman was I that I couldn't keep my husband at home with me? I knew I had to leave, but how would I manage with two small children?

It wasn't too long before I found out I was pregnant again. You may ask why I kept having children with a man who abused me. The answer is that most of the time I was forced to fulfill my "wifely duties" or there would be a fight, so I complied. I did whatever I had to do in order to avoid an altercation. That pregnancy was different from my previous two, however, because I was high-risk. I had to be careful, because I knew Mark didn't care about me and certainly didn't care that we had created another life.

In my ninth month I found out that Mark was cheating on me with a soldier in my unit. Eventually she found out he was married, and I can only assume she said something to him that set him off. When he came home that night he instantly attacked me while I was folding clothes, because he was mad at the situation he had put himself in.

A few days after the fight, I noticed my baby wasn't moving as much as she usually did. I figured it was because I was so close to my due date. When the day finally came for my princess to arrive, I went home to get my hospital bag and told Mark she was coming and that we needed to get to the hospital. He looked at me and said he didn't give a (expletive) about me or the baby and hoped the baby died. I didn't have time to dwell on that statement, but it hurt me to my core. How could anyone be that cold-hearted?

I arrived at the hospital and was admitted then prepped to deliver the baby. When the doctor checked the baby's heartbeat, I noticed he looked distressed. After watching him check the fetal monitor a few more times I was worried. A few moments later the doctor looked at me and said, "I'm sorry, but the baby is dead." I was lost and confused. I delivered her and just held her. She was so beautiful. My soul cried out to God and I asked why this was happening. I called Mark and told him he got his wish, that the baby had died. That was the day I started losing my sense of reality. The pain of losing a child was the worst I had ever felt. Just to know she wasn't here because I chose to stay in an abusive marriage crippled me. Where was my strength? I couldn't even protect my unborn child.

After my daughter's funeral things were normal for a while, but it was really just a nice calm before another storm. For a moment, I thought God had finally answered one of my many prayers for peace in my home. The calm didn't last, though, and it wasn't long before the mental and physical abuse started again. By that time I was completely numb to it all. It didn't matter if he called me names, it didn't matter if he hit me, and it didn't matter if he left me alone to go see other women. I would often lie in my bed and begin to pray and cry out to God to please kill me, to just let me go to sleep and not wake up. I believed that the world would be better off without me in it and that the pain would stop. I asked God what I did to deserve this. Did I not deserve to be loved? The answer to that would come much later. I knew I had to do something and couldn't allow my children to continue to see the black eyes, bruises, and, most of all, the disrespect. I was in such a dark place emotionally and found myself contemplating killing Mark. In my mind, even knowing that if I killed him I would go to prison for about twenty-five years, I had peace, as my mother would get my kids and everything from there would be okay.

God had a different plan for me and I'm glad He did. If not, I would probably be incarcerated to this day. I began to look at myself in the mirror daily and tell myself that this was not how life was supposed to be. I needed to get back to me. But who was I now? I could never be the person I was before. I had forgotten what true happiness felt like. Staying in my shell of a marriage had sucked out every ounce of my joy. I prayed for a change, then I waited. Mark eventually moved to another duty station and I stayed behind. My prayers were answered and I knew the end was near.

I worked hard and saved my money until I had enough to file for a divorce; getting him to sign the papers, though, was a different story. Surprisingly, he signed and was okay—until he received the divorce decree. He read it over and realized he would be paying child support. Mark called and stated that if any money came out of his check he would kill me. I tried to be calm but inside I was terrified. He was so unpredictable. I would find myself calling his house and hanging up just to make sure he was still there and not coming to kill me.

Once the divorce was final, I was lost and confused. Even though he abused me, a part of me still missed him. Starting over was hard, especially with small children, but I had to find my inner strength to survive, not only for myself, but also for my children. I often sat and wondered why God would allow me to be treated this way and asked what I did so badly in life to deserve this, but as I reflected, I eventually realized that it wasn't God's doing, it was mine. I had failed to apply my own principles, the principles that God has given us to live by, to my life.

My children and I were homeless and stayed with a friend for a few months until I was able to get myself together. I finally found a home to rent; I was super excited because it meant the kids would have a place to call home. Life began to feel normal again. I finally had peace of mind. No longer did my body shake when I put the key in the lock because I would never know what I was walking into. Now the kids could be kids and not bodyguards. Even though the actual physical abuse had stopped, though, the effects continued. Even though I was a provider for the kids, I was emotionally dead. I felt as if I had to continually prove myself. I couldn't break because then Mark would have been proved right about me. So I worked two jobs most of the time so we would be okay financially.

I realize now, after the divorce was final, instead of me pretending to be super woman (telling myself I got this and I don't need nobody), I should have immediately gone into counseling. At the time, I felt if I went to counseling it would appear that I was weak. Now, I realize that putting myself into counseling should have been the first thing I did, instead of waiting to do so until many years later. Finally, though, I was talking to a friend and she asked me how I was able to stay in all of that chaos for that long of a period of time. I told her I was broken down to the lowest level and I couldn't leave. I realized at that moment that I didn't love myself. When you truly know your worth, you won't allow anyone to treat you badly.

After going through years of losing friends and losing love, I still wondered what was wrong with me. But I realized that, when I felt someone was getting too close to me, I would push them away. Especially in romantic relationships, I would subconsciously sabotage them—it was a defense mechanism for me. If I didn't allow a person to get too close then they couldn't hurt me too badly. I also realized that, due to my abuse and always feeling like I had no power, I had become very dominating. Not intentionally, but I guess I felt like I couldn't let anyone have any type of advantage over me. I became a very bitter person and, as a result, I messed up several beautiful friendships and relationships. I felt like everyone had a motive and no one could possibly love me for who I am. It took a very special friend to help me see that I didn't have to try to take on the world and that not everyone was going to hurt me.

Ladies, if you're in an abusive relationship, please leave. Be aware that leaving is the most dangerous time, so have a solid plan in place and don't ignore the red flags. Attend counseling if it's available. Be aware of your activities and surroundings. Even though the relationship is over, there is still a great possibility of being harmed during this time. Get as much support as you can from family and friends—you will need it.

It took time, but I learned it was okay to be a little vulnerable. I had been miserable for so long that misery had become my norm. I didn't know how to be happy. I stayed in victim mode for entirely too long. I had no clue that I had closed myself off from the world. I had to decide to break the cycle and find my happiness. It has been a long and slow process, but I am determined. I still have moments where my emotions and thoughts will revisit the past, but I don't stay there. My journey to get back to me will continue.

INNOCENT LOVE VS. GOD'S TRUTH: THE PATH TO POWER, PURPOSE, AND PEACE

by Erika Etienne

At eighteen, some teenagers are exploring their new independence from their parents or enjoying their optimistic views about the road ahead; I, however, was about to make a decision that would change the trajectory of my life. My friends and I were planning our futures and beginning to tread the roads that we had dreamed of since we were children. Some of us were getting ready to depart for college and some of us for the military. Wherever the road would lead us, we knew the world was ours for the taking. I surprised my family with my decision to join the Air Force—something I knew very little about. Inspired by a couple of friends at school and my older sister's experience in ROTC at San Diego State University, I thought it would give me a great opportunity to have a career, go to college at my own pace, and not have to live the life of a broke college student. Although a good student, I was also tired of school work and wanted to travel the world instead. I had a plan to travel while serving our country and getting a nursing degree, and then hoped to cross over into the officer ranks; my realistic and achievable goals met my mother's expectations and earned her stamp of approval.

Four months into my Air Force venture, however, I threw a wrench into my cookie-cutter plan and married a guy that I had met just a few months earlier. We had a whirlwind love affair; it wasn't shaped around anything extremely romantic, but it was just enough to win over my young and naïve heart. He was two years older than me and I found myself intrigued by his outgoing personality and seemingly mature attitude, and I couldn't ignore his edge. He warned me about his bad boy tendencies, but assured me he was turning over a new leaf by joining the Air Force—and, after all, I knew he couldn't be that bad if he was in the military. With both of us being from California, I thought we had plenty in common, with our similar taste in music, laidback mentalities, and love for all things "west coast." He was funny and liked to laugh and have a good time, and I was smitten by his commitment to spending all of his free time with me. I had his unwavering attention—we were inseparable.

Two months into the marriage I was pregnant. I hadn't been out from under my mother's care for a full year before finding myself in full-fledged adulthood, with no knowledge of how to be a wife or a mother. I grew up in a single-parent home, so my example of a wife was the images of the TV wives I admired. I thought if I could cook, clean, pray for him, and keep a smile on his face, then I was doing great; however, I would soon learn that my best wasn't good enough, and that the fun and loving man I planned to spend the rest of my life with would teach me some very tough and life-altering lessons in love.

Early in our marriage, it wasn't unusual for my husband to be away from the house for hours on end. I recall one particular afternoon when he popped up to invite me to a gathering with a few of his friends. I was pleasantly surprised, since most of his outings rarely included me, so I eagerly got dressed to join him. While we were at this gathering, I remember feeling uncomfortable, because the women seemed to know things about him that I didn't. They appeared to be more comfortable around him than I would have liked, laughing and joking in a flirtatious way. I didn't know how they knew him so well, or if I was just being sensitive and insecure. After all, I was five months pregnant and hormonal, so I dismissed my thoughts and did my best to enjoy the afternoon. Later on, one of the girls started dancing provocatively in front of the men, and I must have let my thoughts reflect in my facial expression, because my husband immediately told me we needed to leave. When we got in the car I thought I was free to tell him what I thought of her dancing, but he told me to shut up. Not in so clean of terms, but he let me know he was displeased with my attitude. I was shocked and confused by his demeanor, and couldn't comprehend why he was coming to her defense. We had argued in the past, but he had never spoken to me the way he was during this car ride home—cursing and calling me names. During this exchange, I told him not to talk to me like that anymore, that I didn't feel comfortable with him hanging around those people and I wanted him to stop going over there, especially without me. I guess I must have said too much, because he bashed my head against the car window and told me to shut up again and that I couldn't tell him what to do. I was mortified, as I had never before been yelled at by a man in such a manner and had never been physically assaulted by one either. This was not the guy I fell in love with.

That incident would be the first of many physical attacks, each of them getting worse with time. But compared to the physical abuse, the emotional and verbal abuse would be just as damaging, if not more so. For the life of me, I couldn't figure out how the man I loved so much hated me so deeply. No matter how much I prayed or cried out to God to change him or to make me a better wife, one who he could love, nothing changed. He only grew angrier and more resentful toward me. I was called despicable names. I was told that no one else would ever want me, that I was dumb and stupid, fat, ugly, that my dreams were unattainable, and that I would never be successful. I was his verbal and physical punching bag, often having to walk on eggshells in hopes that I wouldn't say or do the wrong thing to set him off. As my insecurities mounted, my self-esteem depleted, and my sense of self-worth and self-love dissipated. I began to believe every negative thing he said about me. I wore a smile to fool the masses at work and church because I wouldn't dare tell anyone of my embarrassing truth. My daughter and my ability to love and raise her well were the only things I felt were right in my life, but even that was questionable according to my husband.

Despite a move halfway across the country and my prayers for a fresh start, things were still the same, and I decided it was time to accept that we would never have a happy marriage. I was tired of having the police at my house and having to explain my situation to my superiors. I was tired of calling my friends, my mother and sister, and his father with the same story of yet another incident. I was tired of pretending things were okay when they weren't and having to feel like every altercation was my fault—that something I said or did sent him over the edge, and if I just did the right thing then everything would be okay. I hated my life and having to wake up in misery, never sure of the mood he'd be in. There were so many days and nights that I cried in agony because I couldn't figure out why God allowed this to happen and why He wouldn't do anything to change our situation. I wanted to give up, but I knew I had to push through for my daughter because she needed me.

We would ride this rollercoaster for four and a half years before finally getting divorced. It would take one last fight (the first and last time that I physically fought back) and the death of my best friend's mother for me to wake up and face reality. My husband and I had separated a couple of times for short periods, but I could never really let him go. Although the relationship was toxic, I loved him—it was the classic battered woman's syndrome. All it took was a phone call or half-hearted apology for me to let him back in. I hated the thought of my daughter growing up in a house without her father, like I did, but I hated the thought of raising her in chaos even more. The small glimmer of hope I had that my husband would one day snap out of it and love me was never realized. No matter how much I cried, begged, or blamed myself for our problems, he was incapable of loving me. All of the "little drama" he said he liked in order to keep the relationship alive became too much to bear and I had to get out.

In the courtroom, with tears in his eyes, he asked if I was sure about this decision. With tears in my eyes as well, I gave him an uneasy "yes." Even though he treated me terribly, I wasn't sure that I wanted to divorce, as I had hoped deep down inside that he would change and that things would play out differently, but I knew I had to say yes. It was time to walk away once and for all—it was the best decision for all of us.

After our volatile marriage was finally dissolved, God made one thing apparent to me, and that was that my love for my ex-husband had been exalted far above my love for Him. I was more concerned with earning my ex-husband's approval than I was with having a relationship with God. Every tear and every prayer was about changing my ex-husband and fixing our damaged relationship, it wasn't about God changing me or revealing my role in our dysfunction. After being in an abusive relationship, it's easy to solely blame the abuser, but we all play a part in our story. It wasn't until after our divorce that I began to see how significant my own issues were in landing me in such a relationship. I will never excuse or dismiss his behavior; however, I explain this to point out how failing to seek God, and a lack of knowledge and self-awareness, can influence poor life decisions.

The turmoil wasn't just about him lacking self-control, it was that we were incompatible from the start for reasons beyond our control. We both had unresolved issues from childhood—his were rooted in resentment toward his mother, while I was in search of someone to fill the void I had from an absent father. My ex-husband showed me love in a way I had never received before, and I misinterpreted his manipulation, jealous tendencies, and controlling behavior as evidence of his love for me. We wed against the will of our parents and loved ones, who recognized that we weren't at all prepared for marriage or the responsibilities it came with. They knew we weren't ready, but when you're young, you think you know everything and that your elders refuse to support what makes you happy, so you go against the grain.

Neither of us had a strong enough relationship with God to recognize we needed supernatural healing, so we tried doing it on our own and failed. We didn't truly seek God before saying "I do," but instead trusted our gut instincts that we were making the right decision. We were ill-equipped for the task and didn't have an example of a healthy relationship to reference. Couple that with our whirlwind romance, abrupt leap into parenthood, and unrealistic expectations of one another to fit a mold that didn't exist, our marriage was a disaster waiting to happen. Our outward expressions of frustration and what we needed differed in severity, but we were both youth crying out for help that was beyond the other to give.

My world at the time caused me to doubt God's love for me, because I couldn't understand how a God who loved me would allow such horrific things to take place. I questioned whether or not my purpose on earth was to be marred by abuse or to serve as the dumping ground for someone's hurt and rage, or if I was just as pathetic as my ex told me I was. I was powerless, in an environment where I had no voice, no right to an opinion, and no ability to defend myself. My peace of mind was nonexistent.

Before God truly got ahold of my heart and restored me, I went on to find myself in another tumultuous marriage that almost cost me my life; however, the lessons I learned along the way changed the trajectory of my future. God showed me that I lost the divine gifts He promised in His word. Not in the same way you lose your keys, but in the way I misplaced my identity in Christ, by allowing someone else to redefine me. I say "redefine" because God already defined me in His Word, yet my choices were those of someone who had no identity. God gave us free will, and I found myself in those marriages because I trusted my instincts over His will. I was impatient and did not know who I was in Christ.

The Bible says I am God's child, His friend, justified, redeemed, forgiven, brand new, and not condemned. It also says I am free, an heir, accepted, wise, righteous, blessed, predestined, sealed with the Holy Spirit, alive, seated high, chosen, and LOVED, but I wasn't living like it. I had adapted a new identity of unworthiness, defeat, self-doubt, ugliness, loneliness, shame, and guilt. Whatever I was called, I answered to, and submitted to being a woman (or more like a girl) who yearned for love so deeply that she was willing to accept it in any form, and at any cost.

The Bible says in 2 Timothy 1:7 (NLT), "For God has not given us a spirit of fear and timidity, but of *power*, love, and self-discipline," and, in Acts 1:8a, "You will receive *power* when the Holy Spirit has come upon you . . . ." There was a barrier to me receiving the Holy Spirit's power and my life was consumed with fear that was imparted upon me through the tactics of abuse and intimidation. I was completely unable to comprehend how someone with such a miserable life was worthy of anything God had to offer, and I certainly did not feel anything remotely close to powerful. I couldn't see beyond my natural state as a sinful being, couldn't see that hidden within me, in a secret place, was my birthright or power as a believer in Christ and daughter of the King.

From a young age I knew my purpose was to impact the lives of women, but how quickly I forgot in the midst of these challenges. My mother always quoted and instilled in us Jeremiah 29:11 (NLT): "'For I know the plans I have for you,' says the Lord. 'They are plans for good and not for disaster, to give you a future and a hope.'" And Romans 8:28 (ESV) says, "And we know that for those who love God all things work together for good, for those who are called according to his purpose." Those words eluded me, because, at the time, I felt I was in God's will (under my terms), and surely my life was a disaster. How could God use my misfortune and turn it into something good? For the life of me, I didn't understand that, just as God wanted the people of Jeremiah's time to understand He was with them even in their seemingly unbearable situation, He wanted me to know the same. While I walked outside of His will to involve myself with those men, He knew it was only temporary and that the experience would soon be the block I stood on to manifest His purpose for my life.

Colossians 3:15a (NIV) says, "Let the *peace* of Christ rule in your hearts, since as members of one body you were *called to peace . . .*" and 1 Peter 3:11b (NIV) says "...they must *seek peace and pursue it.*" Despite these guarantees, I allowed my life to be consumed with chaos and accepted it as my norm. To be called to peace means we are summoned and attracted to it, but I in no way pursued it. Instead, I delved deeper into my need to please my exes and to find my way into their good graces, which led to even greater disappointments. While I craved peace, I looked for it in their approval of me rather than in the eyes of my Lord and Savior who truly loved me beyond measure. The type of peace we're promised is deeper than human understanding and conditions—it doesn't wane under any circumstances.

As God revealed the gifts that had been in me all along, that had just been dormant, I was finally able to emerge into the woman He had always destined for me to be. One who was able to walk like she's loved, with her head up and shoulders back, unashamed. It didn't come without having to face the harsh reality of the heart issues that dictated my decisions. Everything I desired and needed was and always has been rooted in Christ, planted in me though the Holy Spirit; however, I lost sight of that in my quest to satisfy my human needs. Once I received and accepted these gifts from God, He blessed me with a loving husband and healthy marriage. He also set me on a path to begin sharing my story with other women. As a woman who was chosen by God to be a living testimony of restoration from brokenness, I write to simply remind you that God is the lover of your soul and the great redeemer. My hope and prayer is that every woman will realize who she is in Christ and will receive these priceless gifts in order to walk peacefully in the divine power and authority God gave to her to manifest her purpose.

SOURCES

Unless otherwise indicated, scripture quotations are from the Holy Bible, King James Version. All rights reserved.

Scriptures marked ESV are taken from English Standard Version®. Copyright © 2001 by Crossway, a publishing ministry of Good News Publishers. All rights reserved.

Scriptures marked NASB are taken from the New American Standard Bible®. Copyright © 1960, 1962, 1963, 1968, 1971, 1972, 1973, 1975, 1977, 1995 by The Lockman Foundation. Used by permission.

Scriptures marked NIV are taken from the New International Version®. Copyright © 1973, 1978, 1984, 2011 by Biblica, Inc.™. All rights reserved.

Scriptures marked NLT are taken from the New Living Translation®. Copyright © 1996, 2004, 2007, 2013 by Tyndale House Foundation. All rights reserved.

ABOUT THE AUTHORS

Angela Blair is an internet-savvy health and fitness success coach who has helped countless people transform their personal well-being via her social media, private sessions, programs, and emails. A few years ago, Angela said goodbye to her life in Charleston, South Carolina, in order to live out her dreams and inspire as many people as possible to live in their greatness. She resides in northern Virginia with her daughters, Angel and Jayden, and her two furry sons, Amor and Radar.

Michelle Coleman is a wife, a devoted mother of two beautiful and active boys, and a government contracts attorney in the Washington, DC, area. Michelle received her Juris Doctorate from The George Washington University Law School in Washington, DC, and graduated magnum cum laude at Kent State University in Kent, Ohio, with a bachelor's in business administration.

Michelle enjoys public speaking and has presented on several panels in the government contract bar. Michelle cherishes spending time with family and friends and is delighted to watch her two young boys discover the world.

Michelle's mission is to advance God's kingdom by being a faithful example to everyone she encounters and inspiring them by demonstrating a balanced, holistic lifestyle while raising a family and practicing law.

You can learn more about Michelle and her journey by emailing her at michelle.d.coleman6@gmail.com.

LaSheena Doxley was born in Washington, DC, raised in San Diego, California, and presently resides in Lakewood, Ohio. She is a woman of God, a wife, and a proud mother of six. LaSheena grew up in a multigenerational and blended family home and currently has a blended family of her own. LaSheena is a board-certified, licensed professional counselor through the state of Ohio and currently serves as a counselor at a faith-based organization working with individuals, couples, and families. She obtained her bachelor of arts degree in psychology from Albany State University and her master of arts in marriage and family counseling and therapy from The University of Akron. LaSheena is passionate about making a difference in the lives of others by helping individuals, couples, and families identify and overcome their struggles and disconnectedness in hopes of restoring peace and strengthening relationships.

Learn more at www.fitlyfesolutions.com or
doxley@fitlyfesolutions.com.

Jenell Brown currently resides in Las Vegas, Nevada, and is a full-time employee with the Nevada Army National Guard, where she serves as an environmental specialist. She is a mother of five young men, ranging from ages three to fifteen, and a wife to her wonderful husband, Mario Brown. In her free time she loves playing sports with her boys and working out. Jenell also enjoys reading books that she can identify with, related to the challenges she has with one of her sons. Jenell plans to continue advocating for the right care for her son and to break through challenges that they may have in order to get him the proper care.

Feel free to contact Jenell at nellienellj@gmail.com if you have any questions or comments you would like to share.

Resealia McKinney is married to Roderick McKinney. They had one daughter, Reese Madison, who is their heavenly angel. Resealia was born and raised in Tampa, Florida, and currently resides in Orlando, Florida. She serves God faithfully and desires for everyone she encounters to know Him.

Resealia received her bachelor's degree from Florida A&M University and her master's degree from NOVA Southeastern University. She is a leader, teacher, writer, and speaker. She aspires to impact the lives of women by showing His love for them with the hope they will love Him in return. She is honored to share her story to inspire strength and hope.

She has lived through experiences that provide her the opportunity to relate to almost any situation, as she firmly believes we are all connected through our pain. Resealia's communication style will penetrate the hardest of hearts to hear the gospel message.

Learn more at resealiamc@gmail.com.

Brittany Hogan is a servant of Christ, wife, and Mom of angel babies Niya and Madison Hogan. She also serves her community as an author, speaker, blogger, and founder of Empowered to Conquer, a youth development nonprofit organization. Brittany holds a bachelor of science in chemistry and an associate's as a physical therapist assistant (PTA); she currently serves as executive director of Empowered to Conquer while working intermittently as a PTA.

Brittany's passion is to help others discover and fulfill their God-given purposes and she lives daily to fulfill this mission. The legacy of her daughter Niya, whose name means "purpose," causes Brittany to live each day intentionally, while the peace she gained from her "gift from God," Madison, helps her rely on Jesus' strength each moment. Brittany and her husband, Nick, believe that God will use the legacy of their daughters to reach others for Him.

Learn more at www.authorbnicole.com.

Michelle Wilson is a woman of faith who resides in Virginia with her daughter and has recently started a new chapter in her life as an entrepreneur. She enjoys spending time with her family and friends, including her parents, siblings, nieces, and nephews. Being in the healthcare industry for over twenty years, she has developed skills, abilities, and talents that she is now utilizing to pursue her own ventures, using her love for Christ, her past experiences, and her passion to help women obtain freedom from their own hurts and pains. She is the founder of Date Night with Daddy Ministry: An Intimate Encounter with Our Heavenly Father, which helps women to experience God in a new way, as a loving Father.

To connect with Michelle or learn more about her ministry, you can reach her at michelle@datenightwithdaddy.com or www.datenightwithdaddy.com.

Angel Bartlett is a mother, social worker, activist, and motivational speaker. She spent years in the foster care and juvenile justice system because of physical, emotional, and sexual abuse. That same childhood trauma is what strengthens and empowers her to get back up every time she is knocked down. Angel believes that God continues to keep His Angels on assignment over her life and, like with Job, the devil can do anything he wants but kill her.

Angel helps women and girls from all walks of life conquer their real life and emotional demons, all while continuing to defeat and conquer her very own!

Her favorite scripture is Proverbs 3:5–6 (NASB): "Trust in the Lord with all your heart and do not lean on your own understanding; in all your ways acknowledge Him, and He will make your paths straight."

To learn more about Angel please visit her website at
www.angelbartlett.net.

Tammy Rowe is a very positive and loving young woman and a mother of two beautiful children. She was born and raised in Virginia but currently resides in Atlanta, Georgia. Tammy has a master's degree in nursing and has been a nurse for over ten years.

While pursuing her dreams, Tammy encountered hard times in her life, but she pushed through every obstacle. Working in health care is something she always wanted to do as a young girl, but she had no clue about the troubles that would come with pursuing her dream. These obstacles and challenges brought Tammy closer to God. She began dedicating time in church and praying, and understood that she was not alone in this world. She also learned that some of these obstacles would one day become a testimony to share with the world to help other individuals facing similar situations.

Dana Reed is a native of Washington, DC. She's never veered far from the DC area or her family roots and currently resides in Anne Arundel County, Maryland.

She began her professional career in the eighties, studying electronic technology in Atlanta, Georgia. She later continued her educational pursuits, receiving her bachelor's in information systems management from the University of Maryland University College (UMUC).

Dana enjoys mentoring young ladies, participating in sisterhood groups, and supporting outreach ministries to women through church and community organizations. While the second half of her life appears to be one of new beginnings—a reinventing of self—she believes that it is the light of God shining through to reveal his intended purpose for her life. Her God-given writing style is demonstrated on a variety of topics to inspire the reader and encourage conversation.

Contact her for more information at:
msdanareed@gmail.com.

Evangela Ruffin-Williams is a native of Richmond, Virginia, but currently resides in Charlotte, North Carolina, with her husband, three children, and two grandchildren. She works in the insurance industry and has for over seventeen years. She received her bachelor's degree in business administration from Strayer University in October 2015, graduating cum laude.

She is a Christian who loves the Lord. Her favorite scripture is Proverbs 3:5: "Trust in the Lord with all thine heart; and lean not unto thine own understanding." In her spare time she loves spending time with her family and going on mini vacations or day trips with her husband. Her chapter tells the story of two marriages with one man and how, against all odds, love prevailed through prayer and their faith in God, who they put as the center of their lives.

She can be reached at evangela4664@gmail.com.

Pamela Brunson was born in East Meadow, New York, and was raised in Alabama, where she graduated from Demopolis High School in 1986. Pamela joined the United States Army after high school, where she served on active duty for eight years. After serving in the Army, Pamela worked for the Texas Department of Criminal Justice as a corrections officer at the Lane Murray Unit for twelve years. In 2008, she started contracting in Iraq and currently serves as a security specialist in Kandahar, Afghanistan. She is the mother of three adult children and has two very special grandkids.

Erika Etienne is an author, playwright, professional speaker, and entrepreneur. She has worked with women for over ten years, providing them with mentorship and practical strategies to navigate their lives, and volunteers as a women's ministry leader at her church. Her experiences prompted her to found the faith-based women's group Power, Purpose, and Peace, where she offers spiritual advisement, professional and personal development, and more to women in need.

Erika is committed to helping others put their faith into action and works to exemplify God's love and power. Her life's mission is to share her journey of growth and transformation with others so they can be inspired to answer the call on their lives and fulfill their purpose. In her free time, she enjoys spending time with her family and close friends, reading, traveling, and shopping. Erika lives in northern Virginia with her husband, Marvis, and their three daughters.

To connect, email Erika at erika@erikaetienne.com.

CPSIA information can be obtained
at www.ICGtesting.com
Printed in the USA
FSHW02n0124151018
52940FS